Evaluation of Management and Planning Systems

Nick L. Poulton, *Editor*

NEW DIRECTIONS FOR INSTITUTIONAL RESEARCH
Sponsored by the Association for Institutional Research
MARVIN W. PETERSON, *Editor-in-Chief*

Number 31, September 1981

Paperback sourcebooks in
The Jossey-Bass Higher Education Series

Jossey-Bass Inc., Publishers
San Francisco • Washington • London

Evaluation of Management and Planning Systems
Volume VIII, Number 3, September 1981
Nick L. Poulton, *Editor*

New Directions for Institutional Research Series
Marvin W. Peterson, *Editor-in-Chief*

New Directions for Institutional Research (publication number
USPS 098-830) is published quarterly by Jossey-Bass Inc.,
Publishers, and is sponsored by the Association for Institutional
Research. The volume and issue numbers above are included for
the convenience of libraries. Second-class postage rates paid at
San Francisco, California, and at additional mailing offices.

Correspondence:
Subscriptions, single-issue orders, change of address notices,
undelivered copies, and other correspondence should be sent to
New Directions Subscriptions, Jossey-Bass Inc., Publishers,
433 California Street, San Francisco, California 94104.

Editorial correspondence should be sent to the Editor-in-Chief,
Marvin W. Peterson, Center for the Study of Higher Education,
University of Michigan, Ann Arbor, Michigan 48109.

Library of Congress Catalogue Card Number LC 80-84289
International Standard Serial Number ISSN 0271-0579
International Standard Book Number ISBN 87589-843-2

Cover art by Willi Baum
Manufactured in the United States of America

Ordering Information

The paperback sourcebooks listed below are published quarterly and can be ordered either by subscription or single-copy.

Subscriptions cost $30.00 per year for institutions, agencies, and libraries. Individuals can subscribe at the special rate of $18.00 per year *if payment is by personal check.* (Note that the full rate of $30.00 applies if payment is by institutional check, even if the subscription is designated for an individual.) Standing orders are accepted.

Single copies are available at $6.95 when payment accompanies order, and *all single-copy orders under $25.00 must include payment.* (California, Washington, D.C., New Jersey, and New York residents please include appropriate sales tax.) For billed orders, cost per copy is $6.95 plus postage and handling. (Prices subject to change without notice.)

To ensure correct and prompt delivery, all orders must give either the *name of an individual* or an *official purchase order number.* Please submit your order as follows:

Subscriptions: specify series and subscription year.
Single Copies: specify sourcebook code and issue number (such as, IR8).

Mail orders for United States and Possessions, Latin America, Canada, Japan, Australia, and New Zealand to:
Jossey-Bass Inc., Publishers
433 California Street
San Francisco, California 94104

Mail orders for all other parts of the world to:
Jossey-Bass Limited
28 Banner Street
London EC1Y 8QE

New Directions for Institutional Research Series
Marvin W. Peterson, *Editor-in-Chief*

Contents

Editor's Notes

A long-standing need has existed to address how management and planning systems make a difference in higher education. But organizational research is complex, expensive, and time-consuming. Nevertheless, the evidence on the utility of management and planning systems has been growing steadily over the past five to ten years. Much of it is anecdotal information that appears in case studies. A few major studies have been sponsored, mostly by private organizations such as the Carnegie Corporation, Exxon Education Foundation, Ford Foundation, and the Lilly Endowment, to name a few. The authors contributing to this volume believe that sufficient evidence is now available that the practitioner and executive officer can benefit by reviewing the emergent themes on impacts.

The overall goal of this volume is to collect and synthesize in one place the most important points about the impacts of various management and planning techniques in colleges and universities. The entire issue deals with several outcome-oriented questions. What management and planning techniques have been tried? What are the impacts of these techniques? What contributes to those impacts? How can the executive officer or the practitioner assess impacts on a continuing basis?

Planning has many definitions and meanings to individuals, depending upon the kind of organization involved, the nature of the primary activity of the organization, and the role of a given individual in the organization. Planning is often synonymous with a perspective on management and decision making that emphasizes rationality, utilization of information, and control or influence of future events. Planning may refer to a set of techniques for organizing and analyzing information. Planning may imply an organizational model, an ideal state of the organization, or a blueprint for some future condition. Virtually all of these notions appear in the impacts discussed in this volume.

The discussion is limited to institutional management and planning. All types of colleges and universities are represented in the volume, but there is no attempt to organize chapters around specific institutional types. It is assumed that all institutions face essentially the same basic management questions regarding how to assess what is being done and how to decide what to do. The emphasis is primarily on academic functions, but not exclusively, for comprehensive management and planning systems involve all functions of the institution. This sourcebook does not attempt to cover all types of management and planning strategies. Each chapter does deal with a particular approach, and collectively the chapters sample the entire range of possibilities.

1

Each chapter has four objectives: (1) to summarize briefly current practices and provide references for further investigation, (2) to define and describe what experience and research tell us about impacts in realistic situations, (3) to discuss the conditions that contribute to these impacts, and (4) to suggest some indicators that the practitioner might use to monitor impacts as they occur. Two kinds of impacts are included: changes in specific decisions and related decision processes and changes in the decision setting.

The first kind deals with the intended, tangible, direct adjustments to the way decisions are reached on budget allocations, new program development, or modifications to existing programs. The second kind includes the often unanticipated consequences of changed management operations, which can be both desirable and undesirable. Goal discovery, clarification of norms and values, changed communication patterns, and shifts in information and perceived power are a few examples.

The first two chapters discuss two kinds of strategic planning approaches. Strategic planning, which refers to the organization–environment interface, seeks to establish the fundamental assumptions about the environment, the institution, and the future form of the institution. Cope discusses techniques for assessing the external environment and matching the mission and strengths of the institution to that environment. With an eye on key conditions for success, Caruthers reviews the extensive experience with master plans.

The next two chapters deal with two kinds of tactical planning — management efforts to assure the implementation and achievement of a master plan or a set of institutional goals and priorities and to preserve and improve the vitality and quality of organizational units. Tierney discusses how incentives shape the results of systems designed to establish budget priorities and allocate resources. Seeley synthesizes the extensive experience with different forms of program reviews and evaluations and describes the wide range of results that different viewers have observed.

Management and planning systems are built upon information and analytical techniques. Updegrove discusses the use of a relatively new computer modeling system and outlines why it was developed and why it appears to be more successful than past efforts.

One clear theme that appears throughout these chapters regardless of the approach is the need for strong executive leadership and qualified personnel. St. John presents one particular research-based framework for adding management training and institutional change strategies to the list of commonly practiced planning and management techniques.

In the last chapter, the editor summarizes all the guidelines offered to the practitioner charged with organizing and managing these processes and to the executive officer interested in using the products. Continuous assessment of "How's it going?" is the theme. Finally, all of the contributing authors provide their best two or three references with annotations to help the reader locate the most information about an approach with the least amount of time and effort.

The editor wishes to thank the contributing authors for undertaking the challenging task of pushing beyond a descriptive discussion and dealing with the difficult question of results. Few themes stand out clearly in the often murky evidence. Those that do are important. Those that are more tentative are nevertheless useful to the practitioner and may spur researchers to further study.

Nick L. Poulton
Editor

Nick L. Poulton is director of university planning at Western Michigan University.

Several techniques are available for matching the mission and strengths of an institution to changes in its environment.

Environmental Assessments for Strategic Planning

Robert G. Cope

Postsecondary institutions, like all organizations, exist for one fundamental reason: to serve society. Yet as organizations become successful, they frequently become larger, more complex, often self-perpetuating, and tend to let inside demands engage the energies of policy makers to the near exclusion of what accounts for real effectiveness—adapting to a changing environment. The Roman Empire, the Whigs, and Chrysler Corporation had trouble adapting. Yet higher education, with over 700 years of heritage, has shown a remarkable capacity to accommodate to change while holding to essential values.

This chapter presents an overview and suggests the benefits of some newer, systematic techniques for assessing developing patterns in external conditions. This exercise is stimulating, but difficult because there is no common vocabulary for talking about the environment. The environment is simply an amorphous, residual category, something noninstitutional. Yet if we observe that changes in the environment continually create opportunity and introduce risk, then it follows that advance notice in specific instances is essential to intelligent planning.

Note: The opportunity to prepare this chapter during the summer of 1980 provided by the National Center for Higher Education Management Systems is gratefully acknowledged.

N. Poulton (Ed.). *New Directions for Institutional Research, Evaluation of Management and Planning Systems,* no. 31.
San Francisco: Jossey-Bass, September 1981

Through experience, however, we know how difficult it is even to recognize what is already at work in our socioeconomic environment, and so the prospect of being able to see what is to come may indeed seem staggeringly difficult. Yet there are ways to systematically organize information about the changing nature of external forces, and these methods enhance what is now known in higher education as "strategic planning" (Collier, forthcoming; Cope, 1978; Hollowood, 1979; Shirley, 1979). Essentially, strategic planning matches the mission and distinctive competencies of an institution to opportunities to serve society. Peter Drucker (1980) puts it succinctly: "Planning tries to optimize [for] tomorrow the trends of today. Strategy aims to exploit the new and different opportunities of tomorrow" (p. 61).

The remainder of this chapter reviews techniques used to scan the environment and concludes with observations on how environmental scanning, when directly linked to strategic planning processes, can shape our institutions.

Environmental Scanning

A commonly used "model" for thinking about a 360° scanning of the environment has four dimensions: economic, social, technological, and—increasingly important—political or public policy dimensions (see Figure 1). Policy developments are, of course, among the most critical today. Since pub-

**Figure 1. Conceptual Representation of Environmental
Cross Impacts**

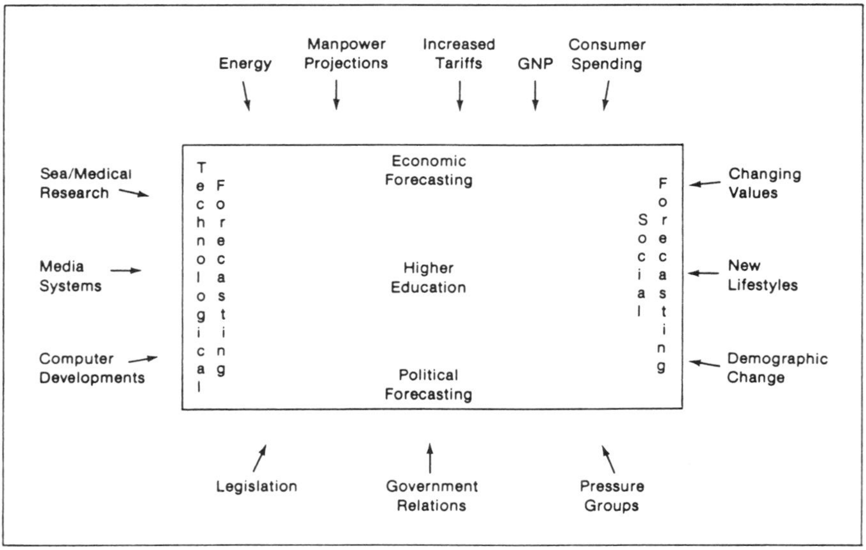

Source: Cope, 1978.

lic policy tends to change slowly and grows through the accumulation of individual events (Kibbee, 1973), an office of institutional research might begin by simply following carefully the new ideas that appear in the literature of higher education, keeping a careful record of those that seem to develop a following.

Reports of some of the larger, more influential foundations can be examined for their ideas and concerns. Likewise, there are certain elected government officials, agency heads, and opinion leaders whose public statements are significant, particularly when certain ideas occur with increasing frequency. Also, the requests of legislative committees for studies can lead to legislation in subsequent years. Certain states tend to be harbingers of change, and thus their public policy decisions, either in the legislatures or in the courts, provide trend indicators. United States Supreme Court decisions provide another source.

The *Chronicle of Higher Education, The Futurist, Change Magazine,* the *London Times Higher Education Supplement,* and editorials, along with major addresses at national conferences, are among important sources of "futures" information. *Educational Administration Abstracts* uses several categories for listing literature reviews that provide sources of forecasts. Examples of useful categories include automation, science and technology, economic development, population changes, and values.

Scanning the 360° horizon by using such categories is likely to reveal a number of ill-defined "blips." To continue the radar analogy, systematic monitoring of each blip on the screen will give policy makers an early warning of possible "missiles," which then become potential opportunities for study, research, and development. Some examples might include: social problems (family discontinuities), community agitation (transport), scientific breakthroughs (minicomputers), emerging social needs (aids for the elderly), economics (productivity), spending (energy alternatives), and education (retraining).

The point is the need for strategic planning to monitor the environment continuously and comprehensively. This can be done through institutional research, or it can be done among cooperating institutions. Probably the best example of continuous cooperative leadership monitoring occurs in the insurance industry under the leadership of the Institute of Life Insurance. It maintains the Trend Analysis Program (TAP), which uses a matrix integrating news from publications on one axis and significant segments of the environment (politics, population, social change) on the other axis. Individual insurance companies are assigned the responsibility to monitor different cells of the matrix for evidence of trends in that segment of the environment. The monitoring companies report regularly to the Institute, which synthesizes their observations.

A similar venture could be undertaken in higher education, where several cooperating institutions could monitor "missiles" and "opportunities" categories, and a single institution could be responsible for summarizing the observations. A national association (such as the American Association for Higher Education or the American Council on Education) could provide the same service in conjunction with an annual conference.

The most carefully prepared scheme for assessing futures related to higher education is the "Futures Creating Paradigm" developed by the Resource Center for Planned Change (1978) of the American Association of State Colleges and Universities. They have developed a four-sided, cross-impact paradigm that integrates (1) national trends, (2) local trends, (3) values, and (4) institutional sectors (curricula, faculty, students, public service, and so on). Their planning is based upon the perspective of the decade ahead, or "planning from the future for the future."

Two Techniques for Forecasting

Given the difficulties inherent even in population projections, forecasting changes in the remaining environment could hardly be called an exact science. That information, however, is subject to even more systematic gathering as already suggested, and is amenable to several forms of display. Two less well-known techniques include probability/diffusion matrices and values profiling.

Probability/Diffusion Matrix. To predict developments over decades, it is useful to think of degrees of relative probability rather than certainty or inevitability. In the final analysis, the assignment of a probability to a trend or future pattern of related events is a matter of judgment, but one based on weighing known data and cross-checking with expert opinion. Part, if not all, expert opinion can be supplied by the faculty.

Cross-checking can be made more exacting by developing a probability/diffusion matrix, as shown in Figure 2, in which predictions are stated along a probability axis so that their relative positions can be made apparent. It is also useful to assess the probable diffusion of a trend or pattern of events as it affects different populations the college serves. The same trends may have different impacts or no impact on different segments of the population. Again, by plotting predictions along a diffusion axis, one makes explicit in a more coordinated fashion the probability of trends and of possible futures. When these two axes are combined as shown in Figure 2, a greater appreciation for interactive efforts and internal consistency can be achieved.

A variation of the cross-impact matrix that allows links directly to an institution's strategic emphases is force-field analysis. In a force-field analysis, the institution identifies pressures (forces) and links them to the institution's planned responses. For example, a community college's planning team recommended four strategic emphases: (1) develop satellite centers; (2) change student recruiting to emphasize not just more but different—more heterogeneous—students; (3) start an in-house faculty development program; and (4) expand

Figure 2. Probability/Diffusion Matrix for Events and Trends Occurring in the United States and World by 1990

Low						Probability			High
Thermo-nuclear war							8 +% inflation		
						30-hr. work week		Minerals extracted from oceans	Rising levels of education
			Sky-trains across both oceans				Energy crises	Less traditional higher educ.	
						Third World relatively poorer			
				Retirement at 55				Multi-national unions	3.5-5% unemployment
	Urban riots		Ecological crises				More business-government partnerships		
		Strikes outlawed				Fresh water crises		Localized solar heaters	$4,500 per capita income
							Regional conflicts		

(Right axis, top to bottom: High — Diffusion — Low)

Adapted from Ian H. Wilson, "Socio-Political Forecasting: A New Dimension to Strategic Planning." *Michigan Business Review,* July 1974, pp. 15–25.

the lifelong learning programs. These emphases responded to certain "forces," as illustrated in the left column of Figure 3.

Values Profiling. A second service for displaying anticipated changes is the values profile. Here we are trying to illustrate changes in sociopolitical value systems. Like the other approaches, this device should be viewed not as a precise measurement (see Figure 4) but merely as one more way to consider changes in the environment. The values profile is made up of contrasting value dimensions (enhancement of one value suggests diminution of the other) that tend to shift as each new generation responds to changing conditions with shifting attitudes. Of course, the change should illustrate the value changes most likely to occur among the segments of the population each college serves — or might serve.

Figure 4 presents value changes likely to occur in the segment of the population higher education has traditionally served — younger men and women coming from homes where there has been a tradition of higher education, of moderate affluence, and of "commitment" to causes. These men and women might be considered the trendsetters, the harbingers of change among other segments of the population.

Two values profiles are illustrated in Figure 4, present and near future. The present line represents the approximate balance struck by these trendsetters in, say, 1980; the future line represents the approximate balance expected in 1990. The location of these balance points can be determined with some

Figure 3. Force-Field Analysis*

Forces ⟶	Strategic Responses			
	Satellite Programming	Recruitment of Different Students	Faculty Development	Life Long Learning
85% Tenured Faculty			X	
Trend Toward Older Citizens in Community		X		X
Declining Number of High School Graduates		X		
Declining State Revenues	X		X	
Long-Term Residential Growth Occurring in Open Lands Away from Central Campus	X			
State and Local Push for Accountability			X	
Facility Capacity Underutilized in Afternoon and Evening		X		X
New Campus Presidential Style as Innovator	X			X
New Types of Industries		X		
Many Closed Elementary School Buildings	X			

*A community college.
Source: Cope, 1978.

Figure 4. Estimating Value-System Changes 1980–1990

Organization		Individual
Uniformity/Conformity		Pluralism
Independence		Interdependence
Sociability		Privacy
Materialism		Quality of life
Status quo permanence routine		Change flexibility innovation
Future planning		Immediacy
Work		Leisure
Authority		Participation
Ideology Dogma		Pragmatism rationality
Moral Absolutes		Situation ethics
Economic efficiency		"Social justice"
Means (especially technology)		Ends (goals)

1978-80 Profile   1990 Profile

Adapted from Ian H. Wilson, "Socio-Political Forecasting: A New Dimension to Strategic Planning." *Michigan Business Review,* July 1974, pp. 15–25.

accuracy through a combination of survey research, using Likert scales, and the Delphi technique, using a panel of experts — perhaps futurists.

Environmental Positioning

A typical feature of the environment is competing institutions. The example of the metropolitan area of Boston, and the position of Boston University in particular, demonstrates what private college presidents know all too well: Institutions must compete successfully to live.

Concentrated in the Boston metropolitan area are nearly sixty colleges and universities, almost fifty of which are private. About 80 percent of the college attendance occurs in the private sector. Boston University, a major private institution in terms of both size (about 40,000 students) and constituent colleges, lies in the middle of America's most college-intense urban environment. Across the Charles River to the north, one sees the spires of both Harvard and M.I.T. To the south is a plot five miles square virtually carpeted with community colleges, a state college, several private liberal arts colleges, business schools, and technical institutes. Boston College is the quality institution for Boston's large Irish and Catholic populations. Brandeis is the impressive, richly intellectual, Jewish-sponsored liberal arts university. Northeastern University, the largest private institution in the country, sprawling and scattered over the Back Bay, dominates higher education's vocational-technical offerings. Tufts University is a smaller version of Boston University with a better-quality image, having its own coordinate college for women. And finally, among the major competitors, there is the public newcomer, the University of Massachusetts at Boston, with a tuition level less than one-fourth that of Boston University.

Boston University, along with its constituent schools and colleges, presents one of the most difficult strategic positioning problems in the United States. Boston University operates one of three independent medical schools in greater Boston, and the University of Massachusetts has started a fourth medical school in Worcester—a reminder that not only do institutions compete, but their constituent units must compete as well. This fact was demonstrated very clearly in competition among California's public medical schools for students and federal funds. It is obvious, then, why Boston University continues to attract a growing proportion of its regular day students from out of state and even targets many of its summer offerings to attract adults from other Eastern and Midwestern urban settings. Meanwhile, the university's president has attempted to minimize the impression that public and private schools are so different that only public institutions should receive tax funds.

Two parts of Rensselaer Polytechnic Institute's (RPI) current strategy illustrate "positioning" in two environments—geographical and technical. Geographically, RPI has chosen to recruit students from three specific urban locations that have both significant Institute alumni and industries using RPI-oriented technologies. These locations are outside the Northeast in the northern Midwest, Southwest, and South of the United States. Technically, RPI has greatly enhanced its computing capability, recognizing this as the basic tool of both the researcher and the engineer. These strategic positions place it in more direct competition with research-oriented graduate engineering schools, yet increase its zones of commitment, thus expanding its market flexibility.

When considering other colleges and universities, it is not necessary to think of them only as competitors. An example of strategic thinking about the place of a school of education in a large university illustrates how a shifting sense of purpose changes the emphasis given to interinstitutional relationships. James Doi, now dean of education at the University of Washington and a founding member of the Association for Institutional Research, presented three alternative strategic perspectives on education: first as a profession, training school practitioners; then as a social science, which draws more on the concepts of the various social sciences; and finally as human development, which serves lifelong processes and draws upon the biological as well as the social sciences (Doi, 1979).

Multidimensional Scaling

A study of twelve public and private colleges and universities in the Pacific Northwest demonstrates the concept of multidimensional mapping (Leister, 1975). The institutions included three public four-year schools, three community colleges, four private four-year schools, one high school with an active vocational-technical program, and one private urban secretarial-book-keeping school. These reflect significant competitors as well as the range of educational offerings to potential students in the Puget Sound region.

The "marketplace" of each institution was found by asking samples of people to tell where they perceived each of the institutions to be on six dimensions: low cost, nearness, size, safety, quality, and offerings. Through a multi-dimensional scaling statistical technique, it is possible to construct aggregate multidimensional perceptual maps, a form of which is shown in Figure 5. Leister's (1975, p. 391) interpretation of the figure follows.

> The University of Washington is viewed distinctly from the other institutions, but is closest to the other four-year state colleges. The four private four-year schools are perceived to be in close proxim-

Figure 5. Joint-Space Map of Institutional Market

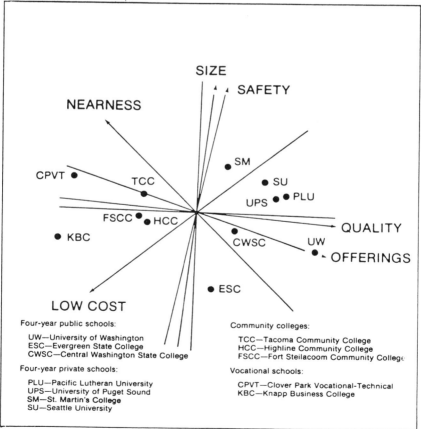

14

ity to one another, as are the three community colleges. At the far left of the figure are found the vocational-technical school and the secretarial-bookkeeping school . . . the figure demonstrates the wide perceptual differences that exist among institutions and types (public/private/academic level) of institutions in competition with each other for the educational dollar in western Washington. For example, psychological distance is greatest between the University of Washington (the largest single-campus university on the West Coast, with some 35,000 students) and the vocational-technical school. Many significant perceptual discriminations appear to exist between and among the twelve institutions. The careful observer will note even significant distinctions between institutions in the same general class, for example, among four-year public schools and among four-year private schools. For example, the educational innovativeness of the Evergreen State College (an open-concept school where students "contract" with faculty members for individualized courses of instruction) appears to have been recognized by the distinctive position it holds in the perceptual space.

The perceptual map can be considered a visual model of the market structure of higher education in western Washington as perceived by this sample of respondents. When constructed from the views of important target markets or persons likely to be influential in choice decisions, the maps can be considered devices for summarizing the degree of competition that exists between the institutions.

Multidimensional scalings with joint space "maps" summarize a great deal of information that can be used in strategy formulations. The market position of competing institutions can be estimated, what is important in determining position on the map is illustrated, and the selection of a new position relative to the competition can be visualized. As Leister points out, these vector maps "can be used as springboards for imagination regarding possible strategy alternatives" (Leister, 1975, p. 397).

Value of the Concepts

Environmental scanning, when employed as a part of a fully participating strategic planning process, offers many interrelated benefits. One might expect these outcomes: help in identifying crucial issues, aid in goal formulation, increased appreciation among operating units for how other units interact with each other and with their shared environment, and increased openness to opportunities. Some obvious impacts — as important as they are easily overlooked — include better communication, focus on direction, and enhanced synergy.

Planning for academic delivery systems and for the coordinating levels of management in higher education will continue to be important because of the need for efficiency. But it is at the institutional level, interfacing with the increasingly turbulent and uncertain environment, that planning has become most important, because of the greater need for effectiveness. Eventual success in strategic planning will depend first on institutional capability to assess the social, the economic, and particularly the political landscape. Then it will depend upon the capacity to deal with constituencies and officials external to the institution, and upon our ability to obtain helpful legislation and positive public opinion. Eventual success or failure now depends on higher education's greater capacity to understand and manage the environment. As Edna St. Vincent Millay said, "There are no islands anymore."

References

Collier, D. *The Strategic Decisionmaking Concept.* Boulder, Colo.: National Center for Higher Education Management Systems, forthcoming.

Cope, R. G. *Strategic Policy Planning: A Guide for College and University Administrators.* Littleton, Colo.: Ireland Educational Corporation, 1978.

Doi, J. I. *Orientations of a University College of Education.* Seattle: College of Education, University of Washington, 1979.

Drucker, P. *Managing in Turbulent Times.* New York: Harper & Row, 1980.

Green, P. E., and Rao, V. R. *Applied Multi-Dimensional Scaling.* New York: Holt, Rinehart and Winston, 1972.

Hollowood, J. R. *College and University Strategic Planning: A Methodological Approach.* Cambridge, Mass.: Arthur D. Little, 1979.

Kibbee, R. J. "The Hazards of Planning—Predicting Public Policy." In R. G. Cope (Ed.), *Tomorrow's Imperatives Today.* Tallahassee, Fla.: Association for Institutional Research, 1973.

Leister, D. V. "Identifying Institutional Clientele." *Journal of Higher Education,* 1975, *46,* 381–398.

Resource Center for Planned Change. *A Futures Creating Paradigm: A Guide to Long-Range Planning from the Future for the Future.* Washington, D.C.: American Association of State Colleges and Universities, 1978.

Shirley, R. C. "Strategic Planning for Higher Education." Paper presented at annual meeting of the American Associaton of State Colleges and Universities, Houston, November 1979.

Wilson, I. H. "Socio-Political Forecasting: A New Dimension to Strategic Planning." *Michigan Business Review,* 1974, *24* (4), 15–25.

Robert G. Cope teaches in the higher education program at the University of Washington, where he specializes in the management problems of colleges and universities.

Extensive experience with master planning indicates that success does not just happen. It requires several important conditions.

Strategic Master Plans

J. Kent Caruthers

One of the more controversial topics in institutional planning has been master planning. Its proponents, largely from the sytems approach school of management, see the master plan as the logical capstone of all planning activity — the grand design for all to follow. Its detractors, however, find that time spent on master planning all too frequently is wasted. Conditions often change to such an extent before the planning period is half over that the master plan becomes obsolete. Which group is right? The purpose of this chapter is to determine why master planning sometimes contributes to, but sometimes detracts from the development of American colleges.

As with many disagreements, part of the problem lies in poor communications among the parties. In this case, there is no accepted terminology for describing what a master plan is, what it is intended to do, or what it should contain. As used in this chapter, the term *master plan* describes a document that includes an expression of the institution's educational and operating philosophy, an analysis of the school's current condition, and a delineation of major strategic changes that the college will implement during the planning period. As used here, the master plan is the direct result of a formal planning process or activity concerned with the intermediate to long-range future of the institution. In various local settings, master planning is sometimes referred to as mission planning, institutional self-study, long-range planning, or, increasingly, strategic planning.

N. Poulton (Ed.). *New Directions for Institutional Research, Evaluation of Management and Planning Systems,* no. 31. San Francisco: Jossey-Bass, September 1981

18

Current Practices and Trends

Few schools will admit that they have not attempted to develop some form of master plan over the past decade. In addition to the almost universal desire to be prepared for the future, many other forces lead to master planning activity: changes in institutional leadership, accreditation requirements, federal program participation, and state higher education board activities. The many reasons for master planning have created a number of approaches. How to develop a master plan effectively and efficiently is a growing concern.

If for no other reason, cost alone makes it important that master planning be performed efficiently. Most master plans are the result of large committees meeting many hours over many months to collect and analyze reams of data. Costs can be staggering. The typical master plan committee is broadly based with administrative, staff, faculty, student, and sometimes lay representation. Kells and Kirkwood (1979) report that such committees regularly meet over a period lasting from twelve to twenty-four months. And, as institutional researchers can attest, master plan committees have a ferocious appetite for data about the institution and its environment—an appetite that often outstrips the ready availability of such data.

Fortunately, nearly all master planning activities—whether conducted successfully or not—are designed in about the same way, at least in terms of representation, scheduling, and analytical approach. This fortuitous circumstance suggests that the alert leader might capitalize on the problem of being required by outsiders to develop a master plan and seize on it as an opportunity to prepare the institution for meaningful change.

Substance of Master Plans. The typical master plan is subjected to a paradoxical set of criticisms: It is at once both too general and too specific. The explanation for these seemingly contradictory charges is that the contents of the master plan range from statements of philosophy and assumptions about the future to exhaustive data listings and detailed timetables. When it deals with philosophical issues and assessments of the future, for which disagreements are bound to arise, the master plan often is worded ambiguously in an effort to achieve accord. This problem, when coupled with the frequently pompous style of academic expression, leads to a master plan that can be interpreted in a variety of ways and that seems to have no focus. As a plan, however, the document also can become almost too specific. Certainly, implementation timetables that are built from projections that are based on other projections will seem ridiculously specific and misdirected once the first projection goes slightly awry. In response to this challenge, master planners are now trying to force choice and clarity in the deliberative phases of the process and to design the implementation steps in a manner that articulates the contingencies that must be met.

Most master planners focus on the intermediate to long-range future, that is, three to ten years. Their scope typically is the entire institution—hence

the term *master*. A master plan will review the institution's history and philosophy of education, analyze data pertaining to institutional operations (enrollments, staffing levels, salaries, costs) and its external environment (manpower
trends, state tax support, demographics), and establish a schedule and responsibility for implementing recommended changes. These recommendations
might involve a shift in mission, such as assuming new research responsibilities. Or the master plan might call for a modified role, perhaps through offering graduate programs for the first time or opening new instructional programs for the professions. Many master plans contain significant detail about
construction schedules and renovation needs. Some of the recommendations
in master plans are for less measurable changes — for higher-quality programs,
for better support services (libraries, campus maintenance), or even for a friend-
lier and more caring work/study environment.

All of these topics can be the subject of other types of plans. When
included in master plans, however, they presumably are to be treated in a
more holistic manner. The impact on, and interaction with, all other types of
institutional decision making is to be addressed. The difficulties and complexities surrounding master planning should be apparent, as should the cause for
the disillusionment of many master planning participants. Nonetheless, a
good master plan can be worth the efforts expended and frustrations produced. The challenge is to achieve the result with the minimum amount of
grief.

Trends. A number of new approaches have been developed to respond
to the problems and disappointments associated with earlier master-planning
efforts. One of the biggest problems with master plans in the 1970s was that
they were never totally implemented or, at least, became hopelessly out of date
from the combined result of leveling enrollments, dwindling resources, and
escalating inflation. A 1973 master plan might have specified some action for
implementation in 1975, but in that year the best (or even perhaps most opti-
mistic) estimate for its accomplishment was 1979. With that kind of track record, it is easy to see why planning participants were reluctant to continue.

More recent master-planning activities have sought to deal with these
problems through being less specific about the target date for a desired action
but more specific about the necessary conditions for its implementation. In
one sense, this approach can be considered a form of contingency planning. It
is less reactionary than contingency planning, however, and resembles the
more practical strategic approach to planning. This approach to master planning seeks to identify what type of match is needed between internal and external factors and then lays out a strategy for enabling this fit to occur.

Another major problem associated with master planning is the sheer
volume of planning activity that needs to occur in one time period. This has
become an even greater shortcoming (in a cost-benefit sense) since implementation plans have become harder to project. The typical institution becomes so
inundated with planning activity during master plan development that insuffi-

cient time is available for each component of the plan to receive adequate attention. A number of large colleges, especially those with well-staffed planning departments, have responded by developing a master planning framework with separate component documents to be developed (or revised) each year throughout a multiyear cycle. In this way, the annual work load is more manageable, priorities can be adjusted annually if the situation demands, and the overall planning document remains more current.

The substance of the master plan, as well as the process for its development, is also changing as a result of the new conditions facing colleges and universities. When master plans came into vogue, their almost uniform theme was growth and development. Now, with only a few colleges having realistic expectations for expansion, master plan topics include the management of decline or, more optimistically, qualitative improvement in the steady state. This change in topics also has led to changes in the types of analysis that need to be performed and the willingness of many to participate. More attention is now devoted to per-student costs, tenure rates, and program productivity than to aggregate enrollment forecasts and capital expansion needs. Potential participants now must evaluate the trade-off between protecting their own interests through active involvement in the planning activity and facing charges of fratricide when other programs must be reduced or eliminated.

Impacts of Master Planning

Both the proponents and the detractors of master planning present a strong case. In some situations, master planning has had positive impact, but in others it has not. A review of the types of impacts that have resulted from master planning can help to focus expectations about future planning efforts. It can also provide insights about which approaches to replicate and which to avoid. Master planning's impact has been felt in decisions concerning program mix and financial priorities. Its impact is seen when an institution enters new markets or renews its sense of identity. The influence of master planning even has an impact on an institution's public relations programs.

Program Decisions. In terms of program mix and emphasis, both positive and negative results of master planning have been seen. At one regional state university, a master-planning decision to emphasize "human services" programs seems to underlie the institution's resurgence. At a different regional state university, a similar decision to become identified as a "polytechnic" institution left the school's constituency confused and its arts and sciences faculty feeling disenfranchised. A residential, church-related, liberal arts college experienced a dramatic increase in freshmen, on-campus applicants as an unexpected (but welcomed) by-product of a master-planning decision to offer more continuing education programs. Yet a women's liberal arts college suffered prolonged internal dissension after its master plan placed greater emphasis on professional curricula. The question is not whether master planning has any impact on program decisions; rather, the issue is how to guarantee positive results from master planning.

Financial Decisions. Likewise, master planning has influenced financial decisions. The efforts of the Albany campus of the State University of New York (SUNY) in preparing for financial cutbacks through strategic planning have been reported by Shirley and Volkwein (1978). Their approach required that each academic support program be evaluated using a number of criteria as the first step in developing a financial reallocation plan. Robl, Karman, and Boggs (1976) described Oklahoma State University's (OSU) thrust in master planning—quality improvement through reallocation. Small proportionate reductions were made in each unit's budget to establish an excellence fund earmarked for achieving planning objectives in higher-priority areas. Not all attempts to link planning and budgeting have met with success. In fact, one can find those at SUNY and OSU who were dissatisfied. A frequent shortcoming cited is the failure to deal with the anxieties of those who are planned into a "lowest-priority" status. Nonetheless, master plans need to be linked with budgets to achieve their greatest impact.

Growth. Master planning need not be limited to retrenchment situations. In fact, careful planning can even help to identify potential new markets and to develop strategies for entering them. Aquinas College, a liberal arts institution facing serious decline, used its master planning effort to identify a number of new opportunities. As President Hruby (1980) freely admits, some of their planned efforts did not work. But the clear conclusion is that master planning helped Aquinas College to survive. When approached with unobstructed vision, master planning can identify unexpected alternatives. A regional university in the Southeast determined that it should expand in a downward as well as in the more common upward direction in the academic pecking order. It sought state board permission to be recognized as the community college for its region in addition to its role as that area's graduate university. Not all opportunities identified in master plans create success stories. Many institutions have misread the signs in the master plan and have wound up weaker than they might have been with no planning activity whatsoever.

Renewal. Institutional renewal is another high-risk area for master planners. Among the more notable successes in this regard has been Austin College. This Texas-based, church-affiliated, liberal arts college did not face serious budget problems before it began master planning. Its budgets usually were balanced, and it managed to attract sufficient numbers of students to impose an enrollment limitation. But quantitative success was not enough, so Austin College successfully undertook a major master planning effort aimed at institutional renewal (Reddick, 1979). A two-year college in Tennessee also found master planning to be a valuable activity for renewing its basic commitments as a community-based institution. Some other attempts at renewal have not met with success. One institution discovered seemingly unresolvable philosophical differences among its faculty when it sought to reestablish its identity as a major teacher-training college. While master planning can yield highly valued benefits, it also has led to divisive attitudes and presidential resignations.

Public Relations. Most of the impacts discussed thus far concern the internal operations of the college. But master planning is also part of a school's external relations program. In some instances, external affairs has been the primary focus of the master-planning activity. Although external relations was not the target of the SUNY at Albany master-planning effort, it did lead to increased public support. University officials report that private parties are more sympathetic to recent fund-raising appeals and that state funders seem more confident of the institution's ability to manage its affairs as a result of its widely publicized planning efforts. A multicampus system in the South generated similar support for a quality improvement program developed through its master-planning activity. The same system, however, found that master planning can become a double-edged sword when its very existence as a system was challenged after dealing unsuccessfully (from the state legislature's perspective) with the competing aspirations of its member campuses for authority to offer prestigious programs.

Master planning undoubtedly has impact, and frequently it has been favorable. But given that master planning has also produced negative consequences — both for the institution and the individual planner — many are understandably nervous about undertaking a major planning effort. They are concerned that the institution may suffer more from master planning than from no planning at all. The key question is how to ensure that master planning will have its intended impact, rather than creating a divided campus.

Conditions for Effective Master Planning

Caruthers and Lott (1981) identify seven considerations in designing a successful mission, role, and scope review. Because master planning and mission review are highly similar activities, those considerations can also be viewed as conditions for effective master planning. They are: determining and developing institutional readiness, clarifying specific uses, organizing for self-study, determining participation, providing analytical support, communicating progress and results, and maintaining visibility.

Determining Readiness. Probably one of the major considerations that characterizes successful master planning is a concern for institutional readiness. Unless the institutional community is ready to undertake the serious deliberations required in master planning, success will be happenstance. Sometimes circumstances create a high degree of readiness, for instance, when a new president is appointed to replace a long-tenured predecessor, or when the institution faces a major external challenge such as a significant drop in funding. At other times, however, master planning may be required even though readiness may be low, for example, when the state higher education board mandates such an activity. Not only must the would-be master planner be able to determine institutional readiness, he or she must also be able to develop readiness when it does not otherwise exist.

Two interrelated factors to consider in assessing readiness are whether there is (1) a positive attitude on the part of those who will participate and (2) an ability to make the necessary commitments of time and dollars. The best ways to overcome any attitudinal problems seem to be ensuring that the results of master planning are needed and will be used, and demonstrating top leadership's commitment through their direct participation. Commitment can also be displayed through the allocation of financial resources. If at all possible, the master-planning activity should not be financed "out of hide" and staffed without release time from other duties. Even small budgetary amounts can change perceptions noticeably. For instance, when Aquinas College financed short field-study trips for its committee members, it enjoyed a tremendous rate of return in terms of increased campus interest in its master-planning efforts.

Clarifying Uses. One of the dangers in master planning is its pervasiveness. Because the master plan presumably covers all aspects of institutional life, anyone who currently has any sort of problem expects that the master plan will provide a solution. For this reason, it is important to be as explicit as possible at the outset about what the planning activity will and will not encompass in order to minimize false expectations.

On the other hand, it can be useful to develop an inventory of what members of the campus community expect to be accomplished by the master plan, and try to accommodate those needs. Aquinas College actually started its planning process with a suggestion box. It frequently will be more desirable to expand the planned effort to respond to one additional need than to find that a similar planning activity has to be repeated the following year. For instance, Austin College expanded its institutional renewal efforts to include its requirements to conduct a regional accreditation self-study. Austin Peay State University linked its participation in the federal developing institutions program with its requirement to participate in several state-level master-planning activities. Through specifying all intended uses in advance, institutions may avoid disappointments, conserve time and dollars, and create a greater likelihood that planning results will be used.

Organizing for Self-Study. A number of conditions for successful planning relate to organizing for self-study: leadership and staffing requirements, decision framework, preliminary assumptions, methodology, and scheduling. Consideration of each of these subtopics is important. It is essential to understand the larger point that time spent in preparing for master planning is well spent.

Of all these concerns, leadership and staffing requirements are probably the most important. Presidential or senior executive-level involvement is an obvious requirement. But the need for strong leaders at the committee and subcommittee levels is sometimes overlooked, even though most of the work is done there. Staffing is also a major concern, especially if much data gathering and analysis is envisioned. When attention is being focused on selecting leaders and staff members, it also is fruitful to determine how decisions are to be made. This is especially important when the planning committee will not have final authority for the decisions at issue.

Another important condition for successful master planning is completing the activity within a reasonable time frame. This can be done through paying attention to assumptions, methodology, and scheduling. Delineating issues and explicating assumptions at the outset can be a big time saver. By determining beforehand that it wanted to remain a liberal arts college and that it only wanted to fulfill that mission more effectively, for instance, Austin College avoided unnecessary debate about establishing a professional school. Aquinas College, which did not have a time constraint but did need to gain broad support, chose a bottom-up approach to master planning rather than using the more efficient top-down method of specifying constraints in advance. SUNY at Albany accomplished much in a surprisingly short period by establishing and adhering to a detailed schedule of activities. Without attention to these factors, a master-planning effort can drag on with serious implications for its chances of success.

Determining Participation. As mentioned previously, most master-planning efforts involve large committees. Participatory governance is part of the tradition of colleges and universities. When master planning is concerned, participation can lead to better decisions and increased chances for successful implementation. It follows that a major condition for successful master planning is determining participation.

Several tenets can guide these decisions. First, every committee should possess the technical expertise — either through its membership or its staff — to address the issues at hand. Second, those who will be most affected by any potential decision need to be represented, especially if they will be expected to implement the decision. Finally, the role of "outsiders" needs to be considered: Can consultants, local citizens, or alumni contribute in any meaningful way? A separate but equally important participation issue is whether the standing governance structure or a special committee will produce better results. No right or wrong approach exists for addressing these issues; rather, a design for participation must be established that fits the style and needs of the institution.

Providing Analytical Support. It is difficult to imagine a master plan without data analysis. Most master plans contain numerous data listings and analyses describing all aspects of institutional operations. Even where the emphasis is not on extensive data collection, successful master plans usually reflect that considerable attention was devoted to understanding institutional history, environment, and operations.

An important but often overlooked aspect of analysis is consideration of the institution's history. In a very real sense, a college's heritage and tradition can greatly limit the degree of change available or desirable. Alumni support, reputation, and operating style are just several of the important factors to be considered. If an institution forgets its past, the danger exists that planned change may be too radical.

Also important (and also often overlooked) is how the external environment shapes the institution. Among the important conditions to consider are economic, demographic, social, political-legal, technical, and competitive trends. Only a small handful of institutions can afford to ignore any of these topics. Analysis for most of these topics does not need to be overly sophisticated to be of value: A major consulting firm in the field does little more than assist its clients in developing lists of the three most important factors in each area (Hollowood, 1979). Where more data are needed, a number of tools and resources are available (Harris, 1978; Makowski, 1979; Peterson and Uhl, 1977).

Information about current institutional operations seems especially important for master planning. Included in this category are enrollment, staff, cost, facilities, work load, and budget information. Together they provide a snapshot of what the institution currently is — its point of embarking on planned change. Most of the necessary information is already collected somewhere on the campus, although it may not be in the format needed for an integrated look at current affairs. One aspect of institutional functioning, however, may not be captured in institutional records. Such intangible factors as morale, quality of decision-making systems, and reputation are not as susceptible to record keeping as are enrollments and budgets, but they are of equal if not greater importance to successful master planning.

Communicating. It may be a coincidence, but most of the schools that have successfully implemented master plans also have had effective communications programs as an important part of their master-planning efforts. These communications programs have included written and oral reports aimed at internal and external audiences. Many of the communications vehicles are newsletters, press releases, published minutes, interim reports, public hearings, and open meetings. Perhaps their real contribution is that no one is caught by surprise with final recommendations and plans. Since most plans require at least some implementation by others, keeping those others informed throughout the planning process is most important.

Maintaining Viability. The final consideration in designing an effective approach to master planning is developing an approach to maintaining the viability of the plan itself. Unless the plan is implemented and remains viable as a day-to-day guide for decision making, the effort generally can be regarded as a failure. One way to help the master plan maintain its value is to monitor both the status of its implementation and the factors that influenced its original formulation. While conceptually simple, monitoring master plan implementation is seldom done, even though many master plans contain specific implementation schedules. Only occasionally is there a concerted effort to monitor implementation through checking to see when tasks are completed and when schedules need to be adjusted. Likewise, little effort is made to monitor those factors that underlie specific plan decisions: the projections, assumptions, and measured opinions that originally influenced recommendations. Monitoring these factors — and proposing modifications in the plan itself when changes occur — could contribute significantly to an effective master-planning process.

Monitoring Master Planning

Although it may seem overly simple on the surface, successful monitoring of a master-planning process requires only two steps. The first is to evaluate the effort against the seven considerations just discussed. For instance, are the right data being collected and analyzed? Is the institution's leadership committed to the process? Are deliberations and issues being effectively communicated? Consulting a checklist of conditions for successful master planning, such as shown in Table 1, provides an easy way to monitor progress.

Table 1. Conditions for Successful Master Planning

Determining Readiness
Are major participants' attitudes supportive?
Are sufficient resources (time and dollars) available?
Does the mission review cycle support planning needs?

Clarifying Uses
What is the primary reason for the mission review?
What other purposes are to be served?
Does the study decision support all intended purposes?

Organizing for Self-Study
Is there sufficient leadership and staffing at all levels?
Is the decision-making process understood?
Do assumptions provide limitations or direction?
Is the methodology appropriate to the resources available?
Does the schedule allow sufficient time?

Determining Participation
What is the role of each campus participant?
What is the role of standing committees?
How will outside participants be used?
Are special task forces necessary?

Providing Analytical Support
How and why has the current mission evolved?
What information is available and needed about the external environment?
    about institutional capacity?
How can the needed data be obtained economically?

Communicating

How should the preliminary study design be communicated?
How will the progress of the effort be reported?
How will the final statement be communicated to internal audiences?
to external audiences?

Maintaining Viability

Who will monitor the need for mission review?
What explicit "triggers" can be set forth to ensure that the mission statement
remains relevant?
How will the new mission statement be used in budgeting? in program planning?
in performance evaluation?

Source: Adapted from Caruthers and Lott, 1981.

The second and, perhaps, more important task in monitoring the plan's development is to determine whether decisions are being made or being avoided. If the participants are seeking the easy answer or reaching a nonanswer through ambiguous wording on important decisions, the process is in trouble. This is not to say that an easy answer is always wrong or that a carefully worded statement is always a deception. But when such actions become the pattern rather than the exception, the master plan is destined to become just another shelf document. When this situation surfaces, it is time to reconsider the first condition — institutional readiness — if the master plan is to have positive impact.

References

Caruthers, J. K., and Lott, G. B. *Mission Review: Foundation for Strategic Planning.* Boulder, Colo.: National Center for Higher Education Management Systems, 1981.

Harris, Y. Y. *Community Information in Education: A Guide for Planning and Decision Making.* Washington, D.C.: National Center for Education Statistics, 1978.

Hollowood, J. R. *College and University Strategic Planning: A Methodological Approach.* Cambridge, Mass.: Arthur D. Little, 1979.

Hruby, N. J. *A Survival Kit for Invisible Colleges.* (2nd ed.) Boulder, Colo.: National Center for Higher Education Management Systems, 1980.

Kells, H. R., and Kirkwood, R., "Institutional Self-Evaluation Processes." *Educational Record,* 1979, *60,* 25–45.

Makowski, D. J. *A Guide to Selected Data Bases in Postsecondary Education.* Boulder, Colo.: National Center for Higher Education Management Systems, 1979.

Peterson, R. E., and Uhl, N. P. *Formulating College and University Goals: A Guide for Using the IGI.* Princeton, N.J.: Educational Testing Service, 1977.

Reddick, D. C. *Wholeness and Renewal in Education: A Learning Experience at Austin College.* Sherman, Tex.: Center for Program and Institutional Renewal, 1979.

Robl, R. M., Karman, A., and Boggs, J. H. "Quality and Vitality Through Reallocation: A Case History." *Planning for Higher Education,* 1976, *5* (5).

Shirley, R. C., and Volkwein, J. F. "Establishing Academic Program Priorities." *Journal of Higher Education,* 1978, *49* (5), 472–488.

J. Kent Caruthers is vice-president for research and evaluation at MGT of America, Inc. Before becoming a management consultant, he was director of strategic planning at the National Center for Higher Education Management Systems and director of planning and analysis at the State University System of Florida.

In the face of conflicting priorities, the incentives built into different kinds of resource allocation processes shape the results produced.

Priority Setting and Resource Allocation

Michael L. Tierney

In the best of all possible worlds, the allocation of resources would follow institutional priorities. In that rational world, a set of priorities would establish the relative importance of various institutional goals for the coming budget period. Resources would then be allocated to those activities according to the priorities. As always, scarcity of financial resources would allow the college to undertake only those activities of highest priority.

Obviously, Pangloss was never a college administrator! The basic conclusion underlying this chapter is that the sequence of decisions easily could be reversed, so that the process by which resources are allocated determines the ensuing priorities. One reason this reversal does occur is the lack of consensus on most campuses concerning what the institution's priorities should be. Do most campus constituencies consider upgrading library acquisitions more important than replacing equipment in the physical sciences? In the face of these conflicting priorities, the incentives built into the existing resource allocation process become preeminent. For instance, if academic departments are not allowed to keep part of their indirect cost recoveries, then that provides an immediate explanation as to why enhancing laboratory equipment in the physical sciences is an institutional priority.

The purpose of this chapter is to review and assess current approaches

N. Poulton (Ed.). *New Directions for Institutional Research, Evaluation of Management and Planning Systems*, no. 31. San Francisco: Jossey-Bass, September 1981

to achieving a more rational system of setting priorities and allocating resources. Three questions are central to this examination:

1. How do the various approaches to setting priorities handle a lack of consensus among campus constituencies?
2. How do the various approaches to improved resource allocation deal with the implied as well as explicit incentives they incorporate?
3. What are the results of institutional experience with the various approaches?

As will be suggested throughout this chapter, failure to satisfactorily resolve the first two questions may substantially affect an institution's experience with these approaches.

Contemporary Trends

It was once fashionable to look to planning, programming, budgeting systems (PPBS) as the means for providing a more rational system of linking institutional priorities and the allocation of resources (Jellema, 1972). However, institutional experience has not tended to fulfill the initial hopes for PPBS (Cammack, 1975; Gillis, 1975; Weathersby and Balderston, 1972). There seem to be at least three reasons for these frustrated aspirations.

First is the problem of developing institutional objectives. Enthoven (1970) summarizes this issue by stating: "I would not waste much time trying to develop an index of total knowledge, discovered or transmitted, in the hope that I could then use it to evaluate alternative programs" (p. 52). This problem is not unique to colleges or universities but has plagued PPBS since it was drawn from developments in systems analysis and operations research. Charles Hitch (1973), long before his tenure as president of the University of California, noted that "The fundamental difficulty is that there does not exist a clear-cut, definitive, operationally meaningful statement of national objectives or of Air Force objectives — even for the present, let alone 1960–1965" (p. 30).

Second, even if it is not possible to quantify the amount of learning that takes place within a college or university, a number of scholars have argued that some form of "policy analysis" could substantially improve decisions (Balderston, 1975; Weathersby and Balderston, 1972). However, Wildavsky (1969) noted that policy analysis tends to be very expensive in terms of "time, talent, and money." Consequently, policy analysis is generally reserved for large-scale, nonroutine planning decisions of colleges and universities. This emphasis upon large-scale problems tends to leave a gap between these problems and the more routine, annual budget planning cycle.

Third, state governments often forced PPBS upon colleges and universities with relatively short notice. The new formats and documentation required to implement such a system tended to harass campus budget staffs already hard pressed to meet deadlines for securing the current year's appropriation. While improved scheduling of the paper flow could relieve some of this pressure, campus budget staffs generally remain skeptical that PPBS will be useful in improving campus decision making.

Setting Priorities. The problems associated with developing definitive, operationally meaningful institutional objectives are reflected in the establishment of institutional priorities for the coming fiscal year. In fact, the immediate resource implications of such priorities probably generate more conflict among campus constituencies than more distant, global statements of institutional goals.

Given this potential for conflict, consensus must be built among constituencies. One major approach to building consensus is the formation of an institution-wide priorities committee. One of the earliest examples of this approach occurred at Princeton University during the early 1970s (Benacerraf and others, 1972). Cheit (1973) also identified such committees as an important institutional response to the new depression in higher education.

A second major approach to building consensus is the management-by-objectives or MBO process. Baldridge and Tierney (1979) point out that most MBO projects on college campuses do not contain the major elements of an MBO program in business organizations. Basically, college MBO programs are planning exercises. Only a few MBO colleges include the assignment of tasks and responsibilities to people within the organization and link employee compensation to how well these tasks and responsibilities are satisfied.

Unlike the priorities committee approach to building consensus, the MBO approach relies upon a more formal structure of authority. Supervisor and subordinate establish a set of priorities for the coming year, the achievement of which is reviewed periodically during that year. The fundamental premise is that subordinate participation in the priority-setting process will ensure his or her commitment to those priorities once they have been negotiated. As might be implied from the "supervisor-subordinate" terminology, the implementation of MBO on campus has been most successful in nonacademic programs, that is, in the registrar's office or in the physical plant.

Within either approach, techniques have been borrowed from the field of organizational development, including the Delphi technique and various team-building activities (French and Bell, 1975). While some of these techniques have proved to be useful on some campuses, it is essential to distinguish between these techniques and the more general objective of building consensus among various campus constituencies.

Efforts to build consensus may either fail or be assumed to be impossible. Colleges and universities have basically two alternatives for making resource allocation decisions when institutional priorities are ambiguous. One is the development of a management control system that gives explicit attention to the variety of markets in which the institution operates. The other is a continued reliance upon explicit bargaining among various interest groups. In reality, both alternatives operate simultaneously.

According to Zemsky, Porter, and Oedel (1978), the large size and complexity of many universities make it impossible to develop a consistent set of institutional priorities. Specifically, they argue that: "Like most complex organizations, particularly those staffed by professionals, the university derives organizational unity from common purpose — in this case, the pursuit of knowledge through teaching and research. *Detailed interpretation of this general ideal, however, is left to academic departments and programs"* emphasis added, p. 233).

In place of detailed priorities, the authors propose a highly decentralized management system in which departments are given a great deal of autonomy to compete within various markets. In some cases, the market test is the ability of the department to attract students. In other cases, it is the ability of the unit to generate external funding. Sometimes it is both. In all cases, those departments which compete successfully will be able to purchase the resources that they require. Those departments which are not able to compete successfully face reorganization, reduction, or elimination.

Apparently, only a handful of colleges and universities are willing to have their departments test themselves in the market crucible. By default, most institutions continue to rely upon internal political processes to determine institutional priorities. At some institutions, this reliance means that the "kitchen cabinet" will continue to allocate resources to those activities which they consider to be most critical. At other institutions, a relatively stable coalition of interests among academic departments will result in routine resource allocation decisions from one year to the next. Regardless of the actual internal process, institutional priorities will rely upon the results of explicit bargaining among various interest groups.

Allocating Resources. A certain amount of parallelism exists between how priorities are established (if at all) and how resources are allocated. It would be a mistake, however, to automatically infer that the direction of causality runs from the former to the latter. Let it suffice for now that solutions to the first tend to be associated with solutions to the second.

By far the most common approach to resource allocation in colleges and universities is incremental budgeting (Caruthers and Orwig, 1979; National Association of College and University Business Officers, 1974). This system of allocating resources focuses on departments and assumes that the current distribution of resources among departments is proper and equitable. Each year, budget guidelines are established that indicate what will be considered reasonable percentage increases in various expenditure categories, such as salaries, travel, and equipment. Even in the situation where college priorities have been established, the budgetary response is typically "an ad hoc determination concerning what increment is needed to effect the programmatic change" (Caruthers and Orwig, 1979, p. 36).

As suggested earlier, an incremental approach to resource allocation is embedded in the campus political structure (Pfeffer and Salancik, 1974; Wildavsky, 1964), and the budget is the record of which interest group prevailed. What is remarkable about most budget processes is the amount of agreement that exists. Although there is grumbling when someone's special request is not supported, the overall level of agreement indicates that a relatively stable political coalition exists at the institution (Cyert and March, 1963). Consequently, the various interest groups do not need to go to war each budget period.

Incremental budgeting has been criticized by a number of individuals who advocate a more rational approach to resource allocation (Caruthers and Orwig, 1979). Initially, such reformers were strong advocates of PPBS. More recently, zero-base budgeting (ZBB) has been taken up as a complement to PPBS in the hope that such a merger will provide the rational system for linking institutional priorities and resource allocation decisions. Specifically, Pyhre (1973) argues that: "macroeconomic planning and policy-making process must be effectively linked with a microeconomic planning and budgeting technique. The hypothesis . . . is that zero-base budgeting provides this microeconomic link to fill the gaps in PPBS" (p. 150).

Pyhre notes that there are two basic steps in ZBB: (1) developing "decision packages" and (2) ranking decision packages. To this may be added a third step, that of appropriating funds for the various decision packages according to some rule (Connors, Franklin, and Kaskey, 1978). In an academic environment, decision packages might be academic degree programs that a college or department would be expected to prioritize in some manner. Resources might then be allocated based upon a full funding of the highest-priority programs, supporting alternative configurations of the program (for example, a shift from a degree-granting to a service program), or some other rule.

One problem with these more rational approaches to linking priorities and resource decisions is the failure to consider the sociopsychological incentives in the process. In the case of ZBB, the idea of providing even a partial ordering of academic program priorities is anathema to most faculty. If the administration persisted, any number of schemes could be devised to ensure that the department continued to receive its usual level of support or to initiate a new degree program without jeopardizing current programs. In other words, once the rules of the budget game are well understood by deans and department heads, it is likely that the original intention of reviewing such programs on their merits will be undermined.

An obvious solution to this problem is to develop a budget system in which the incentives are made explicit and designed to elicit certain desired behaviors. One example of this approach is income–expense budgeting (Adams, Hankins, and Schroeder, 1978; Strauss and Salamon, 1979). In this approach, a college is divided into various budget centers and charged with the responsiblity of generating revenues sufficient to meet anticipated expenditures. In the extreme, every "tub is put on its own bottom," although there are a number of intervening levels prior to this extreme. The fundamental objective is to tie academic planning more closely to fiscal realities by using the budget process to shape departmental priorities.

Impact of Contemporary Trends

A definitive statement of the impact of these trends on colleges and universities must wait until more research-based information is available. Clearly, it is important to identify the academic and financial effects that are emerging. Equally important are the tangible effects, such as the degree of mutual trust among faculty, students, and administrators or the maintenance of an institutional *esprit* and intellectual climate. The experiences of several specific institutions provide a number of emerging indicators of impacts.

Setting Priorities. The formation of a Priorities Committee at Princeton appears to have had a substantial impact on the process by which faculty positions were allocated. First, the committee established a set of principles for guiding decisions to meet projected budget deficits. These principles called for projected deficits to be closed first by increased operating efficiency, second by reductions in administrative and support services, third by reductions in less essential departmental operations, and finally by "selective reductions in particular programs and activities and in some cases by their complete suspension or termination" (Benacerraf and others, 1972, p. 186). Although the range among institutions in recommendations of this kind is substantial, a specific statement of such principles is preferable to the rumors that pervade a campus when reductions must be made to eliminate a deficit.

Second, the Priorities Committee established a set of criteria for evaluating programs and departments. Such criteria are essential to any program evaluation that intends to establish a set of priorities among various academic degree programs. However, it may be the responsibility of such a committee to generate these criteria and discuss the relative weighting of each. (For a more recent and comprehensive list of criteria, see Mortimer and Tierney, 1979).

One outgrowth of similar committees at the University of Michigan appears to be the Priority Fund (Shapiro, 1978). This fund is used to alter the present distribution of funds within the university and to increase long-term support for specific programs. While this fund is financed by a 1 percent tax on the base budgets of all units, these units are able to petition for support from the fund for purposes such as new programs, equipment acquisition, and so forth. Such requests are more likely to be granted if the unit offers matching funds from its own resources.

Shapiro (1978) argues that mechanisms such as the priority fund are essential if a college or university is to recapture some financial flexibility. In a decade that promises to be extremely difficult for many postsecondary education institutions, the development of some financial flexibility is required in order to give the organization time to adapt to changing and unforeseen opportunities and threats. Otherwise, the college is constantly in a mode of crisis management and thus subject to "sudden disruptions in operation which might cause permanent and irreparable damage" (p. 21).

As important as these direct academic and financial effects are, the intangible effects of priorities committees may be even more important. First, they provide a mechanism for assuring the participation of various campus constituencies in these fundamental decisions. In an era in which a wider variety of decisions is being made increasingly by the administration, such committees provide a relatively effective way of making critical decisions without abandoning academic values.

Second, such committees fulfill an important educational function. The campus that is able to consider 10 percent of its operating budget as discretional resources is rare. This lack of flexibility is not well understood across campus. Furthermore, the range of alternatives available to the institution is generally constrained by a number of internal and external (usually political) factors. Again, these constraints are not fully recognized by constituencies. The communication of inflexibility and constraints can occur through priorities committees.

Third, these committees can substantially enhance the level of mutual trust among faculty, students, and administrators. Faculty may well view the formation of such a committee with suspicion, believing that the administration may have a "hidden agenda" that it wants to legitimize. However, a sincere effort to include representatives from various constituencies in an open process can lead to a substantial increase in the levels of trust on campus.

The second major approach to building consensus reviewed in the preceding section centered on various MBO strategies. As previously indicated, MBO on a campus may be primarily a planning exercise, or it may be a total management procedure. Baldridge and Tierney (1979) point out that MBO projects are generally planning exercises. Further, this approach to planning apparently works relatively well. Administrators and faculty report substantial improvement in the planning process at their institutions. Further, this improvement appears to be especially apparent at those institutions that combine this planning process with the institution's information system.

Closer examination of several institutions clarifies what is involved in this focus on institutional planning. Baldridge and Tierney (1979) identify six distinct impacts of these approaches:

1. There was widespread support and acceptance of the planning process itself.
2. The realities and implications of future enrollments and economic trends on the total educational program became better understood.
3. There was greater recognition of institution-wide problems.
4. Interdependency among departments was highlighted.
5. The legitimacy and political acceptability of decisions increased.
6. Faculty attitudes toward planning and governance were more positive.

At the very least, the wide dissemination of a common set of information reduced the bases for conflict. At a few institutions, additional elements of the business

MBO model were also implemented with some success, particularly in non-academic areas. Success in this instance means that most employees are generally satisfied working within these programs. First, it appears that negotiating a set of objectives with one's supervisor substantially reduces the amount of ambiguity and conflict surrounding the determination of which tasks have the greatest priority. Although some may perceive this participation in the goal-setting process as a form of cooptation, the basic fact remains that substantial consensus is achieved regarding institutional priorities in these areas.

Second, the reward structure is clearly defined. Subordinates know exactly the basis upon which they will be rewarded prior to the beginning of the year. Mutual agreement concerning the extent to which goals are achieved generally removes any rancor that one was not fairly remunerated for one's efforts.

Third, there is some evidence to suggest that mid-level administrators are more satisfied with their autonomy and independence under this type of system. Such administrators are able both to negotiate with their subordinates and to reward those subordinates on the basis of their assessment of a job well done. Under some conditions, however, these administrators may also feel that the status of their own positions has declined.

This evidence of success of MBO programs comes from small colleges and universities. The situation may be different in large, complex universities. Consequently, a few institutions have established substantially decentralized management control systems. According to Zemsky, Porter, and Oedel (1978), the initial result of such a system was a transformation in the political dialogue within the university. Specifically, the rules of the budgetary game had changed substantially, and these changes were generally well understood by deans and department heads. One casualty of these changed rules was the School of Allied Medical Professions, which the Board of Trustees voted to phase out over a four-year period (Langfitt, 1977; Mortimer and Tierney, 1979).

Second, academic planning occurred at the level of the schools and departments, not at a university-wide level. With this decentralization came the need to provide accurate, descriptive information on various aspects of each school's operations. As opposed to the complex, nonroutine exercises of policy analysis, these reports were intended to be kept simple and nonpredictive.

Third, a more concrete link was established between academic aspirations and the resources required to satisfy these aspirations. While a more detailed analysis of the income–expense budget procedure will be postponed, it is important to note that, at the University of Pennsylvania at least, "planning builds on control" (Zemsky, Porter, and Oedel, 1978). The incentives built into the budget system shape the types of plans developed by the various schools and academic departments. In other words, the direction of causality in this case is exactly opposite to the more common reconstruction of the planning and budgeting process.

Allocating Resources. Two alternatives to incremental budgeting were suggested in the preceding section: zero-base and income–expense budgeting. Zero-base budgeting has been tried in both academic and nonacademic areas. At least two institutions have attempted to implement ZBB in the academic area: MacMaster University and the University of Tennessee at Chattanooga. The experience at MacMaster has been widely discussed (Caruthers and Orwig, 1979; Gaither, 1978). Three positive impacts have been identified: (1) greater insight into the workings of the university, (2) development of a tougher management approach, and (3) achievement of cost reductions without excessive negative impacts. Negative impacts "included an unbelievable amount of paperwork, the tremendous amount of time required, and difficulty in enumerating priorities" (Caruthers and Orwig, 1979, p. 53). In this latter respect, ZBB would appear to share some of the characteristics associated with PPBS.

At the University of Tennessee at Chattanooga, similar impacts have been noted (Drinnon and Larson, 1980). First, the university identified the following decision package surrounding "people resources": full-time faculty and staff, part-time faculty requests, annual salary increases, equipment requests, and operating budget requests. Second, the administration was able to assign priorities both within each decision package and between packages. In this ranking process, goals and objectives were brought into sharper focus, and the administration was able to explain (and defend) its budgetary actions.

Notwithstanding these examples, a widely shared belief among most observers is that "ZBB is best applied to service and support areas; in academic areas, the fixed costs of tenure allow limited opportunity for reallocation of funds" (Bennett, Owen, and Warner, 1980, p. 21). There have been a number of instances where ZBB was implemented successfully in these nonacademic areas (Caruthers and Orwig, 1979). At Stanford University, ZBB provided the means for reviewing $18 million in expenditures, which resulted in eliminating $500,000 from the budget base and adding $1.3 million in new services (Bennett, Owen and Warner, 1980). In addition, the ZBB process resulted in a clearer formulation of nonacademic program goals and enhanced vertical communication within the university.

It is difficult to separate the effects of income–expense budgeting at the University of Pennsylvania from the decentralized management control system in which it operates. Strauss and Salamon (1979) identify a number of impacts that are more financially oriented. First, the University of Pennsylvania has moved from a situation of operating deficits to a pattern of balanced budgets. Second, the university retains some leverage centrally through a fund not unlike the Priority Fund at the University of Michigan. Thus, the system is not one in which "every tub is on its own bottom," but one in which the administration is able to coordinate and sometimes facilitate the achievement of institutional goals. Third, the use of incentives and allocations from this fund has enabled the institution to implement a "selective excellence" decision rule. On the negative side, Strauss and Salamon offer the following criticisms, which they attribute mostly to faculty members: (1) decisions are made on financial rather than academic grounds, (2) the system creates tension among managers of fund centers, (3) the weight given to enrollments tends to erect barriers to interdepartmental planning, and (4) some fund centers are inherently cost-effective and will therefore get richer.

The implementation of income–expense analysis is not limited to large complex universities. At Clarkson College of Technology, a similar procedure was developed outside the framework of a decentralized, responsibility center management system. Clarkson College is able to identify both the full costs per average student load of each academic degree program and the corresponding revenues. Using this information, Clarkson is able to estimate the unsupported operational costs of each degree program, an estimate that represents "a real measure of dollar resource allocation" (Lindsey, 1976, p. 38). Such estimates are essential if the college is to understand which activities it is subsidizing and to what extent. This information provides the springboard for discussions of whether or not the college should continue to provide these subsidies, discussions that eventually lead to consideration of the importance of such programs to the essential goals of the institution.

The Context for Impacts

This section identifies several basic conditions that influence the type and magnitude of the impacts just discussed. A fundamental premise of this section is that one failure is more instructive than a thousand successes. Even though the nuances as to why a particular approach was successful may be helpful, major pitfalls can be avoided by understanding the mistakes of others. It also seems that for less than successful institutions, if one aspect of a project goes wrong, other aspects will go wrong as well.

Top-Level Administrative Support. Efforts to build consensus or make fundamental changes in the resource allocation process will not occur without the approval of senior administrative officers. Because fundamental changes in the established political coalitions on campus may occur, senior administrators not only must be supportive of the projects, but should be involved in the basic decisions regarding project implementation.

In-House Expertise. All the projects reviewed in the preceding section are heavily dependent upon in-house experts. Such persons combine an understanding of the institution's basic structure, processes, and internal political dynamics with technical knowledge concerning the various aspects of the project to be implemented. Turnover in these individuals is a very difficult handicap for a project to overcome, especially in the early stages of development.

It is sometimes suggested that this expertise can be purchased from external consultants. For instance, these consultants are widely employed in the various approaches to build consensus within the organization. Baldridge (1975) suggests seven rules for ensuring that consultant services are most efficacious in bringing about the desired organizational change. However, no amount of familiarity with the college or university on the part of the consultant can substitute for in-house experts.

In reviewing the role of in-house expertise, one is sometimes left with the nagging feeling that no matter what technique was applied, similar results would occur precisely because knowledgeable and creative persons had already targeted the changes they wanted to accomplish. For instance, a senior-level administrator may identify a need to bolster the campus's overall awareness of the problems and prospects for the 1980s. This administrator then latches on to MBO as a means for achieving this objective, and the desired results occur. The same results probably also would have occurred if a priorities committee had been formed. Thus, it is virtually impossible to separate the influences of such persons from the approaches employed.

Organizational Governance Processes. The setting of priorities and the allocation of resources cut to the core of the academic enterprise. If proposed changes in such fundamental areas are to be successful, then strict attention must be given to the way in which these decisions are reached. Mortimer and McConnell (1978) identify four basic questions underlying these processes:

1. What issue is to be decided?
2. What persons or groups should be involved in the decision?
3. When (at what stage in the decision-making process) and how should such involvement occur?
4. Where (at what level in the organizational structure) should such involvement occur (p. 13)?

It is the third question that should most concern those interested in organizational change. Again drawing from Mortimer and McConnell, six elements of an adequate consultation process are: (1) early consultation, (2) fair and uniform formulation of procedures, (3) adequate time for affected groups to formulate a response, (4) availability of pertinent information, (5) consideration of and response to advice rendered, and (6) communication of the final decision to the affected groups.

Good Information. The role of information has not yet been emphasized in this chapter. In the case of priorities committees, for instance, the various criteria suggested for evaluation of academic degree programs point to specific information that the college must develop. Equally critical is the role of accurate, descriptive information for resource allocation. In the case of the University of Pennsylvania, the entire information system had to be overhauled in order to meet the information requirements of an income–expense budgeting procedure.

It is also important to note that these information requirements tend to be descriptive. Sophisticated cost simulations or financial planning models tend to play a relatively minor role in these approaches to setting priorities and allocating resources. While useful for some issues, such models are generally subordinate to the more general issues involved.

Finally, while good information is essential, it must be timely and concise. Clearly, one of the problems of ZBB (and its predecessor, PPBS) is the production of vast quantities of paper. In an organization where time is a scarce resource, the production of too much information is to be avoided.

Implementation Questions

In implementing projects to alter the way in which the institution either sets its priorities or allocates its resources, three questions are helpful in monitoring project development.

1. Are the functions of the institution's management control system clearly distinguished from those of strategic planning?

Anthony, Deardon, and Vancil (1972) point out that "strategic planning is essentially applied economics, whereas management control is essentially applied social psychology" (p. 8). This distinction is critical to the development of effective management control systems. Clearly, strategic planning is taking on increased importance within colleges and universities. However, the problems tackled in strategic planning are directed toward the long-term financial viability of the institution. Further, these problems tend to be complex, nonroutine, and subject to uncertainty.

Such problems are substantially different from the issues surrounding the establishment of institutional priorities and the allocation of resources from one year to the next. These issues are primarily sociopsychological, having to do with how one builds consensus among individuals or how one organizes the rules of the budget game. As in most organizations, the goals belong to the college, but people must work together to achieve these goals.

In passing, it should be noted that a fundamental element in any strategic plan should be the nature of the management control system that will be required to achieve long-run goals. While the content of most strategic plans revolves around substantive issues (what academic degree programs to offer at what levels), these procedural issues are easily as important. In fact, the turbulence and uncertainty within the postsecondary education environment will probably make academic degree program goals more transient than goals related to the institution's capacity to adapt to changing circumstances.

2. Are the institutional governance implications of the proposed approach to setting institutional priorities clearly identified?

With limited resources, the establishment of institutional priorities is essential. Equally as important is the manner in which they are developed. The intangible benefits of mutual trust and the maintenance of academic values more than outweigh the increased time such committees may require or the political costs of not forming them. The reader is again referred to Mortimer and McConnell's four questions and description of the consultation process.

> 3. Are the incentives built into the management control system understood by deans and department heads?

No system of allocating resources is neutral with respect to the incentives that it offers deans and department heads. The usual treatment of academic departments as expense centers creates a number of incentives. For instance, without the ability to carry over funds from one year to the next, resources are squandered at the end of the year in order to justify resource requests at least comparable to last year's level. There may be nothing inherently wrong with incremental budgeting in its current or a revised form as long as such a process provokes the desired behavior on the part of deans and department heads.

Having the desired incentives in place is one thing; making sure that they are understood is another. A change in the way in which resources are allocated must be accompanied by an educational program for deans and department heads. Good managers will identify the changed incentives quickly enough. Poor managers may not identify these changes as quickly, a delay that may lead to serious harm of the manager's unit.

What constitutes a rational system of linking institutional priorities and resource allocation? Faculty members tend to act in accordance with the incentives they perceive. Designing a resource allocation process that carefully considers the ensuing incentives can stimulate faculty to consider new opportunities. According to Strauss and Salamon (1979): "Faculty members who see objective, concrete incentives for their departments and for themselves take renewed interest in planning and funding efficient educational efforts" (p. 17). As long as these incentives are consistent with institutional goals and priorities, what could be more rational?

References

Adams, D., Hankins, R. L., and Schroeder, R. G. *A Study of Cost Analysis in Higher Education.* Vol. 1. *The Literature of Cost and Cost Analysis in Higher Education.* Washington, D.C.: American Council on Education, 1978.

Anthony, R. N., Deardon, J., and Vancil, F. R. *Management Control Systems.* Homewood, Ill.: Richard D. Irwin, 1972.

Balderston, F. E. *Managing Today's University.* San Francisco: Jossey-Bass, 1975.

Baldridge, J. V. "Organizational Change and the Consultant's Role." In J. V. Baldridge and T. E. Deal (Eds.), *Managing Change in Educational Organizations.* Berkeley: McCutchan, 1975.

Baldridge, J. V., and Tierney, M. L. *New Approaches to Management: Creating Practical Systems of Management Information and Management by Objectives.* San Francisco: Jossey-Bass, 1979.

Benacerraf, P., and others. *Budgeting and Resource Allocation at Princeton University.* Princeton, N.J.: Princeton University, 1972.

Bennett, K. H., Owen, L. S., and Warner, T. R. "Implementing Zero-Base Budgeting at Stanford University." *Business Officer,* 1980, *13* (11), 21–27.

Cammack, E. F. "The Program Budgeting Experience in Wisconsin." In R. G. Cope (Ed.), *Information for Decisions in Postsecondary Education.* Tallahassee, Fla.: Association for Institutional Research, 1975.

Caruthers, J. K., and Orwig, M. *Budgeting in Higher Education.* AAHE–ERIC/Higher Education Research Report No. 3. Washington, D.C.: American Association for Higher Education, 1979.

Cheit, E. F. *The New Depression in Higher Education: Two Years Later.* Berkeley, Calif.: Carnegie Commission on Higher Education, 1973.

Connors, E. T., Franklin, H., and Kaskey, C. "Zero-Base: A New Look at Budgeting for Education." *Journal of Education Finance,* 1978, *4,* 248–259.

Cyert, R. M., and March, J. G. *A Behavioral Theory of the Firm.* Englewood Cliffs, N.J.: Prentice-Hall, 1963.

Drinnon, J. E., and Larson, D. R. "Zero-Base Budgeting: A Public Institution's Experience." *Business Officer,* 1980, *13* (8), 24–26.

Enthoven, A. C. "Measures of the Outputs of Higher Education: Some Practical Suggestions for Their Development and Use." In B. Lawrence, G. B. Weathersby, and V. W. Patterson (Eds.), *Outputs of Higher Education: Their Identification, Measurement, and Evaluation.* Boulder, Colo.: Western Interstate Commission for Higher Education, 1970.

French, W. L., and Bell, C. H., Jr. "OD Interventions—An Overview." In K. N. Wexley and G. A. Yukl (Eds.), *Organizational Behavior and Industrial Psychology.* New York: Oxford University Press, 1975.

Gaither, G. "Zero-Base Budgeting in Higher Education." *Business Officer,* 1978, *11* (9), 18–21.

Gillis, A. L. "Program Budgeting: An Evaluation from Academic Planners, Budgeting, and System Perspectives." In R. G. Cope (Ed.), *Information for Decisions in Postsecondary Education.* Tallahassee, Fla.: Association for Institutional Research, 1975.

Hitch, C. "An Appreciation of Systems Analysis." In S. L. Opfner (Ed.), *Systems Analysis.* Baltimore, Md.: Penguin Books, 1973.

Jellema, W. W. *Efficient College Management.* San Francisco: Jossey-Bass, 1972.

Langfitt, T. W. "Management of Change: Closing a School." Paper presented at annual meeting of the Association for Academic Health Centers, San Diego, 1977.

Lindsey, F. G. *Final Report to Exxon Education Foundation Resource Allocation Management Program.* Potsdam, N.Y.: Clarkson College of Technology, 1976.

Mortimer, K. P., and McConnell, T. R. *Sharing Authority Effectively.* San Francisco: Jossey-Bass, 1978.

Mortimer, K. P., and Tierney, M. L. *The Three "R"'s of the Eighties: Reduction, Reallocation, and Retrenchment.* AAHE–ERIC/Higher Education Research Report No. 9. Washington, D.C.: American Association for Higher Education, 1979.

National Association of College and University Business Officers. *College and University Business Administration.* (3rd ed.) Washington, D.C.: National Association of College and University Business Officers, 1974.

Pfeffer, J., and Salancik, G. R. "Organizational Decision Making as a Political Process: The Case of a University Budget." *Administrative Science Quarterly,* 1974, *19,* 135–151.

Pyrhe, P. A. *Zero-Base Budgering.* New York: Wiley, 1973.

Shapiro, H. T. "Resource Planning and Flexibility." *Business Officer,* 1978, *12* (3), 20–23.

Strauss, J. C., and Salamon, L. B. "Using Financial Incentives in Academic Planning and Management." *Business Officer,* 1979, *13* (5), 14–17.

Weathersby, G. B., and Balderston, F. E. *PPBS in Higher Education Planning and Management.* Report P-31. Berkeley, Calif.: Ford Foundation Program for Research in University Administration, 1972.

Wildavsky, A. *The Politics of the Budgeting Process.* Boston: Little, Brown, 1964.

Wildavsky, A. "Resuming Policy Analysis from PPBS." *Public Administration Review,* 1969, *29,* 189-202.

Zemsky, R., Porter, R., and Oedel, L. P. "Decentralizing Planning: To Share Responsibility." *Educational Record,* 1978, *59,* 229-253.

Michael L. Tierney is associate director of the Higher Education Finance Research Institute and associate professor of education at the University of Pennsylvania.

Although experience with program review and evaluation systems
is extensive, direct impacts on decision making have not met expectations.
However, emerging evidence indicates that program reviews
have many important but often subtle impacts.

Program Review and Evaluation

John A. Seeley

Program review, as used in this chapter, is essentially a management and learning process of systematically identifying and collecting information about a set of related activities that have been developed to accomplish some end. It assumes, sometimes unwisely, that more and better information, effectively collected, recorded, and presented will lead to more informed and, hence, better decision making. Evaluation refers to forming an opinion about the merit and future development of a program. Evaluations take place constantly. However, program review and evaluation used together imply a formal, multistage process that promotes reflection on a series of courses or curricular activities usually resulting in a degree or certificate. Program review and evaluation are used interchangeably in this discussion.

Program review, in its most limited scope, can refer to a process focused on a single unit or program at one point in time. However, the phrase also describes a system of periodic reviews that are linked at the institutional level to other processes, such as budgeting or planning. Program reviews are often thought of as state-initiated processes, but they also originate at the institutional level and sometimes develop from the desires of unit or program leaders.

Program review signals different things to different people. A comprehensive view contains several stages, as outlined in Table 1. Program reviews are sometimes narrowly thought of as stages two, three, four, and attention to these stages is essential. However, by focusing on the other stages as well, the vitality and usefulness of evaluations can be enhanced. Hence, for the pur-

N. Poulton (Ed.). *New Directions for Institutional Research, Evaluation of Management and Planning Systems*, no. 31.
San Francisco: Jossey-Bass, September 1981

Table 1. Stages of Evaluation

Phase	Stage	Activity
Creation	1	Evaluation needs assessment
	2	Evaluation initiation
Implementation	3	Evaluation implementation
	4	Reporting
Utilization	5	Knowledge utilization
	6	Decision implementation
	7	Decision impact assessment

poses of this discussion, program evaluation is meant to encompass these seven stages as grouped into three phases: creation, implementation, and utilization.

The discussion begins with a review of the factors and trends influencing the review process. Then, current options in structuring the review practices are noted. Next, the impacts of reviews are discussed. A limited amount of evidence is available in this area, but the shape and direction of impacts are beginning to emerge. Finally, several conditions related to monitoring the review process are identified, and suggestions for practitioners are offered, divided into the three phases outlined in Table 1.

Factors Influencing the Review Process

Much debate surrounds the need for program reviews. They are undertaken for a variety of purposes. Demands for institutional and programmatic accountability, need for efficiency, promotion of quality, interest in consumer protection, changing demographic patterns, desire for better management, and resource limitations, if not financial exigency, are all factors that promote the initiation of program reviews. These well-documented factors shape the evaluation needs assessment and evaluation initiation stages. The factors that shape the evaluation and implementation and reporting stages have not been as thoroughly identified or discussed. However, three sets of factors seem important to consider: (1) organizational characteristics, (2) individual characteristics, and (3) developments in the program evaluation field.

Organizational characteristics such as faculty and staff morale, institutional autonomy, and the balance between teaching and research shape the receptivity to evaluation. Institutional complexity, size, and norms of centralization versus decentralization condition the implementation of reviews. Leadership stability, the existing management information system, and the professional qualifications of those conducting the review all have an impact on how it is received and utilized by those in the institution.

Individual or personal factors are also important determinants in the implementation and impact of reviews. Individuals have different disciplinary values and different learning, communication, and management styles (Mitroff and Mitroff, 1979). These factors influence the kinds of questions they ask and their receptivity to varying forms of feedback. Preferences for quantitative versus qualitative information are influenced by these styles.

Trends in the professional field of program and educational evaluation influence the nature of the review process. New evaluation models, techniques, and approaches outside the traditional experimental paradigm are appearing and gaining acceptance as evaluators and institutional researchers have become more experienced and better trained. The field is considerably more conscious of knowledge utilization than it was five or ten years ago.

Two additional issues are important to remember as factors influencing reviews. First, systematic program review is a relatively new phenomenon in higher education. For faculty members and administrators accustomed to peer reviews and accreditation visits, systematic program reviews initiated at the state level, the system level, or the academic vice-president's office represent a change in the status quo and are sometimes threatening. Therefore, institutions and systems are struggling to find new ways of accomplishing evaluations. The old equilibrium has been upset by new needs necessitating new practices. Some institutions have established a new equilibrium, others are just beginning the change process. Generally, the situation is in flux.

Second, the review process may represent a general but psychologically difficult attempt to establish limits in our society. In contrast to the expansive 1960s and 1970s, we are in the throes of adjusting to limited purposes, limited numbers of "traditional" students — in their late teens or early twenties — limited energy resources, and limited financial resources. This condition will not evaporate in the near future. Therefore, program reviews and evaluations become one mechanism for reflection and adjustment in times that call for exactly that.

By blending these factors and other issues, four trends appear to stand out. First, the retrenchment of higher education, as we currently know it, will continue as a reflection of broader social trends in a society recognizing limits. Therefore, the pattern of increased program reviews initiated especially at the state and institutional levels will continue as one management response.

Second, reviews will continue to take many different forms in the near future as the general concept is applied by different people in different settings. This trend reflects the reality of diverse circumstances and the breakdown of the "scientific" paradigm as the preferred knowledge-seeking approach to evaluation.

Third, those involved in program reviews will gain increased knowledge about the processes and its impact. This practical and research knowledge will be applied to improving review processes in general, and institutional practices in particular. Generally, institutions will feel less threatened by the process as more experience is gained, and procedures are realistically adjusted.

Finally, there will be increased attention to issues of knowledge utilization. As reviews and evaluations meet the additional tests of relevance, credibility, and utility with various audiences, better professional practice in the area of utilization-focused evaluation will emerge.

Many contextual factors and the trends mentioned are somewhat distant from the institutional researcher. Further, they are largely out of his or her control. They will, however, continue to influence the number, kinds, and value of program evaluations in both the public and private sectors. Some organizational and personal factors are easily within the influence of the practitioners. Understanding one's setting and recognizing that users of reviews are adult learners (Knowles, 1978) are key ingredients in the successful implementation of program evaluation.

Current Options in Review Practices

Purposes and practices for program reviews vary tremendously across the country. This review of the range of practices demonstrates the many options and, therefore, the many important decisions necessary to make regarding program reviews.

Purposes. Three broad purposes shape most program reviews. The first deals with basic program planning information — developing information about program needs and installation. The second focuses on program improvement or modification — adjusting the program to its goals or environment. The third is concerned with program justification — developing information for certification, accreditation, or continued funding.

More specific purposes are shaped by the needs of those initiating the review. Melchiori (1980) identified five clusters of issues that shape reviews initiated by state agencies (see Table 2). Leaders at the institutional level are faced with resource allocation questions and often need comparative data on program productivity, quality, and cost. Faculty at the program level need detailed improvement and impact-oriented data that analyze the educational process. Open participation at the design stage for individuals at various organizational levels tend to expand purposes and, therefore, to make the review process more comprehensive, valuable to more people, and less threatening. However, it also becomes more complicated, time-consuming, and costly to design and implement.

Focus. The focus on the evaluation can be thought of in at least three ways. Focus through definition involves creating an acceptable definition for the term *program.* Narrowly defined, a program is a series of courses leading to a degree or certification. Broadly defined, a program is a set of related activities developed to accomplish some purpose. Focus by concentrating on new, yet-to-be-implemented programs, existing programs, or both is another way. A third way is through conceptual focusing. The evaluation literature contains many conceptual models. One model emphasizes program context, input,

Table 2. Reasons for Conducting State-Level Program Reviews

Date-Related Issues	Program-Related Issues	Quality-Related Issues	State-Level Issues	Institutional Management Issues
Develop enrollment statistics	Develop program descriptors/typologies	Establish quality standards	Overcome program proliferation due to earlier segregation	Change institutional attitudes; create retrenchment awareness
Identify activity level indicators	Establish realistic program inventories	Assess accreditation review problems	Resolve public versus private program rivalry	Induce faculty/administrators to leave; encourage attrition process
Collect data on staffing patterns (faculty and support staff)	Identify special program features	Study feasibility of geographic distribution of doctoral programs	Change institutional thinking/planning into state planning	Establish program discontinuance coping mechanism, for example, retraining, relocating systems
	Modernize curricula	Establish quality control mechanisms	Encourage inter-institutional planning	Reverse institutional decentralization regarding programmatic and budget matters
			Synthesize institutional missions into one higher education state plan	Identify special institutional missions and enforce such delimitations

Source: Melchiori, 1980.

implementation, and outcomes as four distinct elements worthy of evaluation. These four areas suggest different decision-making needs, from program planning to accountability. It is difficult for evaluations to be all things to all people. Also, the educational process is diffused throughout an institution, and its effects are both immediate and long-term. Therefore, agreeing on a focus and accepting its merits and limitations is an important element in the design process.

Initiators. Program reviews can be mandated or encouraged from several different organizational levels or perspectives (Feasley, 1980), including the legislature, the state agency, the multicampus system, the institution, the accrediting agency, or the department. Regardless of who initiates the review, the issues are (1) how best to structure the design and implementation of the evaluation so an infrequent process can efficiently meet the knowledge needs of people at different organizational levels and (2) how best to ensure meaningful involvement of program faculty and administrators in the evaluated unit so the data are valid, credible to them, of value to them, but also meaningful to individuals more distant from the program.

Evaluation Designers and Implementors. Often, the individual who initiates the review is not the one who designs it in detail or implements it. Potential designers and implementors include faculty and staff from the organizations just mentioned, such as state agencies, systemwide offices, central offices in a university, and college or department offices. Another group of designers and implementors includes external reviewers. Peer reviewers from specific disciplines, accreditation teams, and professional evaluators are used as outside resources. Also, individuals internal to the institution but external to the program are used to design and implement evaluations. Sometimes, designers and implementors represent a mixture of individuals from various groups.

Intensity and Process Alternatives. Intensity refers to the depth of scrutiny involved in the evaluation. Process refers to the way the review activities are conducted. Evaluations are conducted at two basic levels of intensity. Flagging refers to a highly quantitative review that identifies programs with problems by someone's definition. Low-degree productivity is one criterion used to flag programs. In contrast, comprehensive evaluations or reviews usually utilize quantitative and qualitative criteria and provide considerably more information. Often, these two levels of intensity are used together to identify and then explore programs that are singled out by initial screening criteria.

Choices in the process used to design and implement a program review are outlined in Table 3. Three choices deal with design alternatives, and six deal with implementation alternatives.

Criteria. The criteria used to establish, change, or justify a program grow out of particular needs and circumstances. Establishing consensus on criteria, especially if they are to be applied to several programs, is difficult because of our dual values of encouraging equality while maintaining diversity.

Barak and Berdahl (1978) identified seven major factors used by state

Table 3. Process Alternatives

Design		Implementation	
Open◄──────►Closed		Comprehensive◄─►Selected	
(all relevant parties)	(key decision makers)	(all program aspects)	(key information needs)
		Cyclical◄──────►As needed	
		(every 5 years)	
Extensive◄──►Limited		Uniform◄──────►Diverse	
deliberation	deliberation	(same criteria)	(different criteria)
		Open◄──────►Confidential	
Complete◄──►Emergent		Independent◄──►Integrated	
(at initiation)	(as issues arise)	(of planning and budgeting)	(with planning and budgeting)
		Systemwide◄──►Single unit	

Source: Adapted from Mims, 1978.

agencies in their review of new programs: program description, purposes and objectives, needs analysis, availability of adequate student financial aid, cost analysis, resource analysis, and program accreditation.

For existing programs, Barak and Berdahl (1978) cited the Education Commission of the States Task Force on Graduate Education as proposing that state agencies use the following ten criteria.

- The number of graduates from the program in each of the last five years
- The number of students enrolled in the program, plus entry and dropout rates
- The size of classes and the cost of courses identified as integral elements in the program
- Cost per program graduate
- Faculty work load
- Program quality as reflected by its regional or national reputation, faculty qualifications, and the level of position achieved by graduates of the program
- Total number of program graduates in similar programs from all institutions in the state, region, and/or nation
- The economics and/or improvements in quality to be achieved by consolidation and/or elimination of the program
- General student interest and demand trends for the program
- The appropriateness of the program to institutional role or mission.

The use of qualitative and quantitative criteria in program reviews is often hotly debated. Melchiori's (1980) literature review and empirical work uncovered nine criteria frequently used for program reviews. The four quantitative criteria are: number of graduates per year, enrollment in program as a major, credit hour production, and faculty work load. The five qualitative criteria are: type of employment found by graduates, faculty quality, comparisons with similar programs, student quality, and quality of curriculum. These criteria imply different methods and approaches to the review process. Measurement in some of the qualitative areas is and will continue to be a difficult task.

Methods and Models. The methods and models used for program reviews should reflect the purposes and, therefore, the research questions or criteria shaping the review. They will also reflect the professional and monetary resources available for the evaluation, the values of those initiating and conducting the review, and the time constraints of the review process. Generally, high-level administrators want broad indicators of program performance, while program practitioners desire more detailed information on impact, needs, strengths, weaknesses, and the causal forces behind learning increases, student retention, and satisfaction. These different starting points imply different models and methods. For methodological reviews and discussions, see Anderson and Coles, 1978; Feasley, 1980; Gardner, 1977; and Stufflebeam and others, 1971.

Users. Program review users can be placed in four basic groups: supervisors, practitioners, participants, and interested others. Supervisors have some management relationship to the program. Their role may be as department chairperson, dean, academic vice-president, president, central system administrator, or state agency official. Frequently, they need to compare programs through the review process. Practitioners within the program include faculty members, advisers, or administrators who each have their curiosities and decision-making needs. They prefer detailed information about their particular program or responsibilities. Future, current, and past participants include students, graduates, or prospective students who are interested in the nature and quality of the educational experience. Interested others may be faculty members, parents, legislative staff, or a host of other people who do not have to make current decisions based on the review. Nonetheless, these individuals are curious about the results of the review.

Identifying user groups helps to shape the information distributed in one or several forms and forums. The next step is to determine how members of these groups best receive information or more broadly how they learn. Approaching them as adult learners (Knowles, 1978; Mitroff and Mitroff, 1979) provides a body of theory and practice that can contribute to enhanced utilization.

Impacts of Reviews

Very little systematic research is available on the impact of program reviews in postsecondary education. This is true at both the institutional and state levels. As late as 1978, Barak and Berdahl (1978) wrote, "We know of no studies which have carefully examined the costs and benefits of program review" (p. 83).

Limited information on the impact of program reviews is consistent with a general lack of systematic research on the results of the evaluation process in many educational and social settings. However, attention to this area has increased substantially within the last few years, as evidenced by the increasing number of studies reported in the literature. (See Patton, 1978, and Weiss, 1980, for their own results and extensive bibliographies.) Regretfully, much of the evidence to date indicates that the direct or instrumental impact of evaluation studies on decison making is minimal. However, research is used in a variety of other ways that eventually influence action (Weiss, 1980). Information on the total impact of program reviews in higher education is limited because too much emphasis has been placed on the relationship between the review process and program discontinuance. Program discontinuance is only one result of program reviews. Also, research in this area is politically sensitive, and information is often hard to gather (Melchiori, 1980).

Nonetheless, some research across postsecondary institutions (Dougherty, 1979; Melchiori, 1980; Mingle, 1978; Poulton, 1978), case study evidence (Arns and Poland, 1980; Greenberg, 1978; Gubasta, 1978), and personal experience suggest findings in two areas. First, we can decipher the nature of the impact. That is, we can determine at what levels it occurs, what changes in institutional processes result, and how the programs under review are affected. Second, we can discern what characteristics of the review process seem to lead to specific outcomes. Important impacts also occur at the individual or program, institutional, and system levels.

Program Level. Program reviews can focus on new or existing programs, and the observed impacts for each are different. New programs that are well justified can be developed immediately, developed in phases, or postponed. If justification is not substantiated by the program review, the proposal is not considered further. For existing programs, Melchiori (1980) found four categories of impacts, each of which contained a variety of possibilities, as presented in Table 4. Although considerable overlap is possible among the impact categories of modification, merger, and termination, the terms do reflect the range of different decisions and intentions contained in program review impacts.

Another intended impact on existing programs for reviews initiated at the state level and at the institutional level is improved quality (Arns and Poland, 1980; Gubasta, 1978). Therefore, changes are expected to occur in degree and major/minor requirements, curriculum content, the number and sequencing of courses, course materials, new educational experiences, teaching style, improving test procedures, student retention, and student entrance requirements. Little systematic research has been conducted to determine if qualitative improvements have taken place across all these areas. Experience suggests that they have.

Table 4. Program Review Impacts

Continuation	Modification	Merger	Termination
Contingent continuation	Changes in structure of program	Merger: internal	Degree granting authority elimination
Conditional continuation	Changes in curricular design	Merger: external	Specific degree elimination
	Changes in mode of delivery	Merger: generic	Paper program elimination
	Budget reductions	Merger: thematic	Inconsequential program elimination
	Additional appropriations	Consortia	Consequential program elimination
	Elimination of subspecialties	Intercampus rotation	Unit/department/college elimination
	General phase-down		

Source: Adapted from Melchiori, 1980.

Program reviews can result in no change or in a great variety of changes. They tend to legitimize and speed already apparent actions, rather than discover needed actions (Poulton, 1978). Sometimes these changes are linked to broader institutional planning and resource allocation processes. The use of memoranda of understanding between program level and central level officials is one way of linking reviews specifically to these processes.

Institutional and System-Wide Levels. Institutional and systemwide impacts are similar and tend to be linked to broader processes such as budgeting, planning, and accreditation. Impacts in specific cases can vary, given that reviews can be single-unit ad hoc, institution-wide, one-point-in-time, or cyclical. Seven major types of impacts, along with specific examples identified in the studies cited earlier or from personal experience, are listed as follows:

1. *Clarification of Missions*
   • Goals were made explicit and congruence at the institutional, program, and individual levels was facilitated.
   • Program priorities were clarified.
2. *Communication*
   • New lateral relationships were created.
   • A forum for discussion of issues based on the same information was created.

- More information and understanding was communicated within the institution.
- Deans and directors became aware of the information on which decisions were made.

3. *Institutional Processes*
   - Budgeting was linked to planning and specific performance expectations.
   - Decision making was improved because credible information from a variety of sources was brought together at one point in time.
   - A general change process was stimulated because new information on needs and performance became available.
   - The planning process was stablilized, even though the leadership changed, because memoranda of understanding linked to the review process were honored.
   - The institutional research process was improved and legitimized because relevant data were collected, disseminated, and used for decision making.

4. *Institutional Credibility*
   - Program review provided a process and symbol for accountability.
   - The process made performance and problems explicit for potential student consumers to evaluate.

5. *Institutional Flexibility:* Monies for potential reallocation were located.

6. *Institutional Climate*
   - The review process increased receptivity to critical self-analysis.
   - Participation in rational change was facilitated.

7. *Institutional Management:* Having more information on needs and performance, administrators were in a better position to coordinate internal affairs and articulate their positions.

Reported by Barak and Berdahl (1978), the following comment by a provost exemplifies a number of these results.

Our experience with the reviews encourages me to think that it is possible, even in an institution with a strong tradition of faculty distrust of administrators, both to have a successful series of assessments at a finite point, and to intensify receptivity for ongoing self-assessment. We achieved a good deal immediately. Positions were eliminated and reallocated with communal assent. New needs were located, some of which were satisfied in the following year's budget. But even more significant was the attempt to create a new mood. Despite the seeming threat to the faculty, the review process can ultimately reinforce the faculty by focusing so centrally upon it. Seldom is the college faculty member the subject of such intensive professional scrutiny, except during tenure

56

reviews. Rarely does the campus faculty as a whole go through a common professional experience. If the process of scrutiny is potentially supporting as well as potentially threatening, and if the faculty becomes self-critically a participant in the process, then the base for continual self-assessment should have been established [p. 85].

It should also be noted that the review process can have a variety of negative impacts, such as the following:
- Time and effort are wasted because more data are collected than can be productively used.
- Viewed as inherently threatening and negative, the review process creates unwarranted anxiety.
- Leadership credibility is diminished because the information requested is not used, or its use is not made visible enough.
- Distrust is created because the uses of the information are not conceived and articulated clearly enough from the outset, report confidentiality is not clarified, or the various roles in the process are not adequately determined.
- Inaccurate information causes unwarranted embarrassment or pride.
- Attention and time are diverted from the teaching, research, and service functions of the institution.
- Resentment arises because the process is not designed to be useful at the program level as well as at higher organizational or system levels.
- The review leads to raised expectations for resources that are unavailable, which causes disappointment.

Poulton's (1978) work in major research institutions noted general impacts and specific results at the unit level, college level, and central level. Generally, he found that:

The primary benefit of a program review process is the opportunity that it provides for structured introspection where information is collected, assembled, analyzed, and communicated in ways that do not normally take place through the standard practices of most operating units. Much of the information collected is not necessarily new. The primary value lies in the assembly of diverse information at one point, in one place, reviewed by parties in different locations in the institution, and subjected to a series of well-structured questions, which form the heart of the program review process [p. 6].

More specific impacts at each level are described by Poulton in Table 5. His distinction of single-unit reviews versus the accumulation of reviews has many implications. It suggests different purposes, which imply differences in scope, timing, participants, and users.

Table 5. Typical Impacts of Program Reviews

Organizational Level	Relative Utility	Nature of Change
Unit Reviewed (department program)	Greatest utility (primarily from a single review)	Increased introspection Revised objectives for teaching and research Better-organized qualitative and quantitative information Clarified unit/program goals, strengths, and deficiencies Improved unit procedures Improved contact among unit members Improved rationale for resources Potentially increased frustrations
School/College	Moderate utility	Improved information on unit trends and priorities, strengths, and weaknesses Better indications of unit quality and responsiveness Adjusted college policies and procedures Adjusted resource decisions (occasional) Adjusted organizational structures (occasional)
University Administration	Least utility (requires accumulation of reviews)	Revised institutional policies and procedures Major organizational changes (rare)

Source: Poulton, 1978.

In general, Poulton's (1978) findings on the impact of reviews in higher education are quite similar to Weiss's (1980) in mental health and Patton's (1978) in health evaluations. Evaluation research and program reviews are used in a variety of subtle, noninstrumental ways, in addition to being applied to a limited number of major decisions. Information from a variety of sources, including program reviews, accumulates and provides a context for the gradual emergence of decisions by policy makers, program faculty, or student consumers. Therefore, the impact of the review process can be expected to be more diffuse and incremental than obvious and dramatic.

Conditions and Procedures Affecting Impact

Writing about their experiences at Ohio State University and the University of Vermont, Arns and Poland (1980) "found that the way in which a review is conducted is at least as important as why it is done" (p. 280). Specific choices among the design and implementation alternatives mentioned earlier in Table 3 make a difference. Also, several conditions in the institutional environment contribute to the usefulness of reviews. These include: leadership stability and continuity; a climate where the initiation of the review process is motivated primarily by a desire to improve the quality and management of the program or institution, not by political or financial exigency; and receptivity to the potential usefulness of the review by the personnel in the program being evaluated.

Within a conducive institutional environment, the experience of several observers indicates that many issues need attention to enhance the initiation, implementation, and utilization of program reviews. The following list of suggestions represents these issues:

- Invite participation from a wide spectrum of information users during the design and reporting stages of the evaluation. At the design stage, the point is to seek advice, not to make a commitment to respond to everyone's curiosities.
- Recognize that the introduction of systematic reviews builds on existing informal reviews. Therefore, they are extensions of processes already in place.
- Undertake an evaluation needs assessment, and develop realistic expectations and parameters for: the impact of the review process, the amount of data to be collected and eventually reported, and the amount of staff time at the program level and central level required to implement a review. Remember to ask the question, "What if we didn't conduct this review?" (Heydinger, 1978).
- Create positive incentives for undertaking reviews, especially in a period of retrenchment when program merger or discontinuation is one possibility.
- Ensure credibility of the process by involving respected faculty and competent staff.
- Consider the review process more as an adult learning/teaching exercise than as a research and presentation exercise.
- Educate faculty and administrators as evaluation consumers on the potential of evaluation, so that their curiosities and concerns are used to shape the evaluation process.
- Use a flexible, responsive, and adaptive approach to the review process. While respondent confidentiality is crucial, open access to aggregated results should be encouraged.
- Recognize the importance of continued, not only initial, visible top leadership support of the review process.
- Use multiple criteria in evaluating program performance.
- Recognize the importance of good internal communication regarding criteria, roles, and responsibilities in the review process.
- Provide periodic feedback to the program's personnel on the status and results of the review.
- Utilize peers at the same institution to check the clarity and objectivity of the review. Use them also to disseminate results.
- Provide review results in several forms and in several forums.

A formal program review process is also a program to be reviewed. For example, it is helpful to assess the timeliness of a review, to determine the usefulness of the process, and to gather ongoing reactions so that improvements and adjustments can be made to the process, and impacts of the process can be enhanced. Therefore, the issues raised about program reviews throughout this chapter are also relevant for a review of the review. The review process may be simple or complex in scope and depth; but, in any case, program review, institutional research, and planning staff need to attend to "reviewing the review." Effective assistance in this task can come from an internal faculty/staff committee, from an external consultant or research group, or from some combination of these. By carefully considering what you want to know and the options available to you, solid information can be developed to assess the management of program evaluation.

This chapter has reviewed the contemporary context and some recent trends within it that affect program reviews or evaluations. Current options among purposes and practices have also been identified. The impacts of the review process on programs and the institution have been discussed. Individual programs are affected through improvement, modification, merger, or discontinuance. Programs are often left unchanged, but validated. Institutions are affected because of changes in priorities, communication patterns, budgetary processes, and planning activities. If not well designed and conducted, however, reviews can consume considerable resources, exacerbate tensions, and possibly diminish the credibility of top-level administrators. Reviews may best be understood more as contributions to a general knowledge base for administrators, faculty, students, and state officials than as "right answers" for specific anticipated decisions or pending actions.

References

Anderson, S. B., and Coles, C. D. (Eds.). *New Directions for Program Evaluation: Exploring Purposes and Dimensions,* no. 1. San Francisco: Jossey-Bass, 1978.

Arns, R. G., and Poland, W. "Changing the University Through Program Review." *Journal of Higher Education,* 1980, *51* (3), 268-284.

Barak, R. J., and Berdahl, R. O. "State-Level Academic Program Review." Report No. 107. Denver: In-Service Education Program, Education Commission of the States, Feb. 1978.

Dougherty, E. A. "What Is the Most Effective Way to Handle Program Discontinuance?" In *Current Issues in Higher Education, No. 5: Assessment.* Washington, D.C.: American Association for Higher Education, 1979, pp. 25-34.

Feasley, C. E. *Program Evaluation.* AAHE–ERIC/Higher Education Research Report No. 2. Washington, D.C.: American Association for Higher Education, 1980.

Gardner, D. E. "Five Evaluation Frameworks." *Journal of Higher Education,* 1977, *48* (5), 571-593.

Greenberg, B. "Program Evaluation Conducted Through an Office of Institutional Research: An Approach, Some Results, and Many Implications." In R. H. Fenske and P. J. Staskey (Eds.), *Research and Planning for Higher Education.* Tallahassee, Fla.: Association for Institutional Research, 1978.

Gubasta, J. L. "Research and Planning Through Department/Program Review: A University Experience." In R. H. Fenske and P. J. Staskey (Eds.), *Research and Planning for Higher Education.* Tallahassee, Fla.: Association for Institutional Research, 1978.

Heydinger, R. B. "Does Our Institution Need Program Review?" Paper presented at annual forum of the Association for Institutional Research, Houston, May 21–25, 1978.

Knowles, M. *The Adult Learner: A Neglected Species.* Houston: Gulf Publishing, 1978.

Melchiori, G. S. "Pattern of Program Discontinuance: A Comparative Analysis of State Agency Procedures for Initiating and Implementing the Discontinuance of Academic Programs." Research report. Ann Arbor: Center for the Study of Higher Education, University of Michigan, 1980.

Mims, R. S. "Program Review and Evaluation: Designing and Implementing the Review Process." Paper presented at annual forum of the Association for Institutional Research, Houston, May 21–25, 1978. (ED 192 629)

Mingle, J. R. "Influencing Academic Outcomes: The Power and Impact of Statewide Program Reviews." In M. C. Fincher and others, *The Closing System of Academic Employment.* Atlanta: Southern Regional Education Board, 1978.

Mitroff, I. I., and Mitroff, D. D. "Interpersonal Communication for Knowledge Utilization." *Knowledge,* 1979, *1* (2), 202–218.

Patton, M. Q. *Utilization-Focused Evaluation.* Beverly Hills: Sage, 1978.

Poulton, N. L. "Program Review and Evaluation: Integrating Results into Decision Making." Paper presented at annual forum of the Association for Institutional Research, Houston, May 21–25, 1978. (ED 181 791)

Stufflebeam, D. L., and others. *Educational Evaluation and Decision Making.* Itasca, Ill.: Peacock, 1971.

Weiss, C. H. "Knowledge Creep and Decision Accretion." *Knowledge,* 1980, *1* (3), 381–404.

John A. Seeley is president of Formative Evaluation Research Associates (FERA), Ann Arbor, Michigan. FERA, founded in 1973, is a nonprofit tax-exempt research group performing evaluations for postsecondary institutions.

*Recent experience with a user-controlled interactive modeling system
indicates that some but not all of the long-standing problems between
modelers and decision makers have been solved. Successful modeling,
however, requires good design, careful communication, and
executive commitment.*

Using Computer-Based Planning Models

Daniel A. Updegrove

Despite widespread and frequently harsh criticism in the last decade, computer-based planning models for colleges and universities appear to be enjoying a
resurgence. This resurgence is the result of the confluence of five factors: institutions' current need for improved decision making, the learning about the do's
and don'ts of modeling that has taken place during this period, the widely publicized success of modeling at Stanford University, the improvement in model-
ing-system software, and, finally, the availability of new delivery systems.

About the demographic, economic, physical, and political problems
facing colleges and university administrators, little need be said here. As docu-
mented annually by Halstead, and Minter and Bowen, monthly by the *Business
Officer,* and weekly by *The Chronicle of Higher Education,* policy makers are faced
with a plethora of trade-offs subject to both increasing resource constraints
and increasing uncertainty. Although management science textbooks would
characterize this an an ideal environment for modeling, so many modeling
efforts have failed miserably that it is surprising to find the leadership of basically conservative institutions turning to models. Today's models, however, are
different from previous approaches — in conception, development, and use.

The Promise and Problems of Planning Models

A model is a synthesis of known facts, theories, and judgments into a
meaningful pattern that represents some real-world reference system (Hop-

N. Poulton (Ed.). *New Directions for Institutional Research: Evaluation of Management and Planning Systems,* no. 31.
San Francisco: Jossey-Bass, September 1981

kins and Massy, 1981). The model is usually quantitative, with a set of user-specified inputs and assumptions ("exogenous" variables), a set of output results of interest ("endogenous" variables), and a set of equations or decision rules for generating outputs from inputs. Although it may be computerized to speed up the calculations (often with loss of control and clarity for anyone not skilled in computer manipulation), the model itself is nothing more than inputs, outputs, and equations.

Planning models of an organization have as exogenous variables both organizational policies and external factors. This makes them ideal for "what if" analyses: "What if inflation increases by a percentage point a year for the next three years?" or "What if we raise tuition by $300?" or "What if we keep salaries even with inflation?" Although attention is usually focused on these planning variables, the validity of the model depends on the often-overlooked equations that determine the changes in the outputs as functions of the what-ifs. All too often, critical scrutiny of a model ceases when it produces a plausible "base scenario" (the result of the set of most likely inputs), whereas the real test of a model is how its outputs respond to changes in the planning variables. Once constructed, a model should be able to display a wide range of what-ifs at high speed and low cost. Some planning models are also programmed for goal seeking—for example, "What enrollment level would balance next year's budget?"—but rarely do they optimize in the sense of "What is the best student-faculty ratio, all things considered?"

Critiques of Packaged Planning Models. Most of the discussion of planning models in higher education has focused on the large packaged models for resource allocation and prediction, namely RRPM, CAMPUS, and SEARCH. In fact, a reader of volume nine in this series, *Assessing Computer-Based Systems Models* (Mason, 1976) would be led to believe that these three models and their European counterparts were the only extant models worthy of discussion. As is well known by now, these models are based on the "induced course load matrix," which displays courses taken by majors and offered by departments. If the data to construct such a matrix can be collected (often a heroic task), and if the matrix coefficients are stable from year to year (often a heroic assumption), the models can be used to examine the impact of changes in enrollment patterns as well as program decisions on the instructional operation.

The expense of data collection, the technical support required to operate these models, and the lack of insight into noninstructional areas provided ample fodder for a number of critics (Hopkins, 1971; Plourde, 1976). In fact, similar large, rigid, data-intensive, and technically complex models met with similar criticism in the areas of national postsecondary education planning (Dresch, 1975), urban planning (Lee, 1973), and public policy analysis (Greenberger, Crenson, and Crissey, 1976).

Much of the blame for the ineffectiveness of models has been ascribed to the wide gulf between modelers and policy makers. Modelers tend to be trained in engineering, economics, and operations research, all fields well known for quantitative rigor and intolerance for the ambiguity and "irrationality" of organizational behavior. As Keen (1977) points out, operations researchers have sought increasingly sophisticated optimization models long after organization theorists like Herbert Simon (1957) observed that decision makers do not optimize, and political scientists like Charles Lindblom (1959) argued that they should not optimize. Thus, Schroeder (1977) states unequivocally: "The only good way to ensure that the focus stays on the larger goal (decision making) is to maintain user involvement. Administrators should be in charge of the systems design effort, not at its mercy" (p. 106).

Custom-Built Models. Schroeder's prescription for custom building policy models is especially appropriate if the administrator is also a systems designer. For instance, former Dartmouth president John G. Kemeny, a mathematician and computer scientist, built successful models for faculty appointment and promotion rates, assigning faculty billets to departments, program options for year-round operations, and endowment management (Kemeny, 1973). Bloomfield at Oregon State (1977), Strauss, Porter, and Zemsky (1979) at the University of Pennsylvania, and countless others have combined in one person or one group the dual talents of administrative and model-building skills.

Perhaps the best-known modeling team has been at Stanford University. There, provost William Miller; vice-president for business and finance William F. Massy; senior staff associate, now assistant dean for administration of the medical center, David S. P. Hopkins; associate provost for budget and planning Raymond Bacchetti; and research assistant, now director of the American Council on Education (ACE) Financial Condition Project, Nathan Dickmeyer, produced a series of budget planning and faculty flow models that have been both successful at Stanford and widely publicized (Dickmeyer, Hopkins, and Massy, 1978; Hopkins and Massy, 1981). It seems clear that modeling succeeded at Stanford because the models were developed in response to the need for solutions, the entire group of top budget officers was involved, and all models were kept small and simple. Often overlooked, however, is the team's expertise; among the members were Ph.D.s in computer science, economics, and operations research.

The Stanford modeling process could not be imitated easily, nor could the Stanford models be applied directly in other institutions, as was discovered by administrators at Harvard, Lehigh, Oberlin, the University of Pennsylvania, and the State University of New York (SUNY) at Albany. These five institutions participated in a feasibility study under EDUCOM auspices to determine the applicability of the Stanford models in other environments. In each case, the models had to be programmed to fit the data, organizations, and decision-making styles of the test sites before they could be useful. Moreover, in each case the model required the support of a key executive during its development and use (Wyatt, Emery, and Landis, 1979).

But what of institutions whose administrators are not systems designers? Either they have had to learn about programming languages, compilers, and the like, or they have had to rely upon computer center personnel or consultants (or perhaps the proverbial "gifted" student). Given the demands on their time, they usually delegate the project, only to learn that the staff are busy on payroll or affirmative action reports (or that gifted students have little patience for documentation). Is it any wonder that we find so many remnants of custom-built models, some that never worked and many that worked only when their designer (who has long since left) was at the controls?

A New Approach: Interactive Modeling Sequence. If packaged models do not allow for user involvement in their design, and custom-built models force the user into systems design as well as model design, a logical compromise is the so-called modeling system or modeling language, which provides a content-free structure within which users can custom build models. Such systems typically provide a matrix that holds data values, flexibility for the user to label the rows (variables) and columns (time periods), a format for specifying a set of equations (either in program subroutines or tables), and a convenient facility for changing the values of the planning variables and displaying the results.

Many people will recognize these as attributes of HELP/PLAN-TRAN, an early modeling system (Midwest Research Institute, 1972) that has been, unaccountably, characterized as a model in much of the literature (for example, Plourde, 1976). HELP/PLANTRAN was an innovation; its relative lack of acceptance can be attributed to two factors: It was bucking the tide of the large resource allocation models, and it was a punch card batch-processed system. All such planning systems are now interactive, operated at terminals connected to time-shared computers or (more recently) to standalone microcomputers. Examples of currently available modeling systems include MAPSS (Planning Management Services Group, 1979), EMPIRE (Applied Data Research, Inc., 1978), VISICALC (Personal Software Inc., 1979), and the EDUCOM Financial Planning Model, EFPM (Jones, Merrill, and Orcutt, 1980).

EFPM: Uses and Users

EFPM, developed by EDUCOM with grant support from the Lilly Endowment, appears to be the most widely used modeling system in use in higher education. EFPM is based on the Stanford TRADES model and, like TRADES, enables users to display alternate forecasts, seek "feasible" policies (those that do not violate any user-defined constraints), and graph policy trade-offs. The widespread use of EFPM is attributable in large measure to the delivery system chosen by EDUCOM. Rather than installing the software on local computers, EDUCOM has opted to make EFPM available over telephone networks to one host computer at Cornell University. Users thus avoid the delay and expense of local installation and maintenance while taking advantage of electronic communications to other users and the central consulting staff (Jones and Updegrove, 1978).

Since its public release in August 1978, over 100 colleges and universities in the United States, Australia, Belgium, and Canada have subscribed to EFPM. Subscribers include large and small, public and private institutions, and applications are found in central administrations and subunits. Despite its origins in a private univeristy, EFPM is used most extensively at Purdue, where applications include legislative budget requests, computer center indirect cost recovery, clerical and service wage parity, and financing of the student hospital, recreational gymnasium, and parking facilities. Since the content of the data matrix is not limited to financial categories, EFPM has also been used for student- and faculty-flow models. Users of the system include chief business officers, chief academic officers, budget officers, institutional researchers and planners, faculty, and graduate assistants. Many of the users have no previous computer background (Bloomfield and Updegrove, 1981; Updegrove, 1981).

Impacts. In a recent survey, EFPM users were asked to indicate the significant benefits (if any) of their modeling application. Only a few reported that the model resulted in different decisions. For instance, the tuition rate at Carnegie-Mellon is apparently higher than it might have been because the tuition committee was persuaded through the use of the model that a larger increase was needed to offset the assumed inflation rate (Knodle and others, 1979). What of the others? Although the system was rated highly by most users (over 75 percent reported that the time and money invested were justified, and over 90 percent of first-year users renewed their subscriptions), it seems clear that changed decisions per se are not perceived to be the critical impact of modeling.

The benefit most frequently cited was the ability to consider more alternatives. Related benefits cited frequently were more accurate analyses, more consistent assumptions, and more consideration of the future. These benefits fit the traditional concept of rational choice as cited by Hopkins and Massy (1981), namely, models increase the sense of intellectual control that administrators have over the institution.

The second most frequently cited benefit was "Building the model forced us to understand the nature and structure of our problems," followed closely by "We ask better questions." Such responses are consistent with what has become almost conventional wisdom about modeling, as noted by Keen (1977, p. 43), "The analytic perspective may thus be the most valuable . . . in clarifying existing knowledge." March (1971, p. 10) goes farther in arguing that "Human choice behavior is at least as much a process of discovering goals as for acting on them." Thus, many modelers have claimed success for models that never were run to completion because learning took place in the model construction process. Cynics have often pointed out that most of the learning was by the modeler, rather than by the decision maker. In the case of this survey, however, decision makers cited this benefit as often as modelers did.

Finally, many modelers responded, "We communicate better with each other." This also is a common claim for modeling, especially in higher education, with its high regard for mutual understanding. In particular, models appear to be able to communicate the financial dynamics of colleges and universities to faculty and students much better than financial statements.

Likely Future Trends. Three interconnected trends are now apparent: increased usage, increased need for communication, and improved delivery systems. After an institution or an individual has had a successful modeling experience, it is likely that other policy/problem areas will then be modeled. Examples include expanding a budget model to include fully detailed models of endowment income and student aid expense, as well as disaggregating a university budget model into its component colleges. As the number of models and modelers increases, so, too, does the need for automated model linkage, electronic mail, documentation standards, and the like. In addition, interinstitutional communication can be expected to improve, as modelers seek both better models and comparative indicators of financial health (Updegrove, 1978).

As modeling becomes less of an exotic research and development activity and more of an administrative utility, pressures will build to increase response time, enhance graphic display capabilities, and provide access to administrative data bases (Keen, 1980). Thus, the next generation of modeling systems can be expected to include microcomputer work/display stations linked to larger mainframe computers. The technology will provide more power at less cost. The key question will continue to be: "Is anyone better off?"

Preconditions for Successful Modeling

Because of the diversity of modeling system applications among a heterogeneous group of colleges and universities, it is impossible to prescribe a set of procedures that will guarantee success. Several common themes do emerge, however, from the literature and the EFPM user survey.

Executive Commitment. First and foremost, there must be top-level commitment to the model. A similar requirement has been postulated for the success of management information systems by Wyatt and Zeckhauser (1975). It is not enough for an executive to authorize the acquisition of software or the commitment of staff. He or she must be willing to get intellectually involved in the construction and operation of the model. This does not mean that the executive must sit at the terminal; but it does mean that the substantive thrust, the choice of primary planning variables, the basic equations, and report formats must be understood.

The executive is usually a vice-president, although he or she may be the president in a small college. The actual computer terminal work is usually performed by a staff person reporting either to the executive or to an "interpreter," such as the director of institutional research. In some instances (Haverford, Oberlin, Swarthmore), the vice-president has done all the modeling work with no staff assistance.

As modeling proliferates within the institution, the same general rule applies: Each model must have its executive "godfather." The actual modeling is sometimes performed for all by a central modeling consultant (for example, Purdue), is sometimes decentralized (Stanford), and is sometimes performed by subunit staff with help from a central staff (Georgetown). Questions regarding the best forms of intermodel communication are too new to have ready answers.

It has been hypothesized that one other aspect of executive commitment is at work with modeling systems that require nontrivial institutional expenditures. EFPM out-of-pocket expenses for the first year average $5,000, whereas RRPM can be purchased for about $100. Hence, vice-presidential (or presidential) approval was required to begin the modeling process. Consequently, the executive had to be convinced of its value before making the decision. The executive and his or her staff will thus have a much greater incentive to get their money's worth. EDUCOM staff speculate that had external funding permitted disseminating EFPM for free, the number of users would have been larger, but the proportion of successful applications would have been significantly lower.

Technical Considerations. Although much of the foregoing has been an argument for modeling as a process, there are some specific technical guidelines for building the model itself. First, the model should be as simple as possible without sacrificing completeness on important issues. Hopkins and Massy (1981) argued that if one cannot understand a model well enough to derive its results by hand, then its use for policy planning is probably irresponsible. Output formats must be familiar to decision makers: A finance committee used to seeing "student fee revenue" will be disoriented with results on "tuition income." Input formats and labels are only slightly less critical. For example, it is much better to have a variable named "Tuition" than one named "X(211y1)." Finally, the model should be adaptable to changing circumstances and conceptions of the problem. Because a new technical staff assistant is not likely to know which policies and problems to anticipate, even these technical guidelines argue for the inclusion of the executive in the modeling process.

Monitoring and Assessing Impacts

Implicit in this survey is a set of criteria for monitoring the impacts of models. First, there is a set of objective criteria: Is the model finished? Is it comprehensible to key people? Is it used by planners and decision makers? Some criteria may be ambiguous. For instance, if the model's structure is changed frequently, it could mean that new insights are emerging, or that errors are being corrected (or both). It is a good sign if decision makers request new scenarios or entire new models.

68

It is usually difficult to determine that a decision has changed because of the model. It should be possible to observe that more alternatives are being considered, that more long-range implications are being considered, and that more fine tuning is being done. Improved understanding of problems should be apparent in discussions, debates, and questions, especially questions from previously uninvolved or naive parties.

Finally, there are some criteria for identifying unsuccessful modeling processes. If only one person in the institution understands the model, if all the debate focuses on the validity of specific assumptions (for example, the inflation rate) rather than on the likely impacts of changes in the assumptions, or if there is no debate at all, then there is a serious problem. Perhaps the most pathological symptom is the statement, "The model made us do it" (Watkins, 1980). If the key people do not understand that the model is merely a tool for improving decision making rather than a substitute for decision making, then modeling will be a disaster.

Interactive modeling systems offer nontechnical administrators the ability to create adaptive models of their organizations. The model is not likely to be correct or useful, however, unless it is the result of a participatory modeling process headed by a key decision maker. As such, modeling can lead to optimality, but only if optimality is understood to be not a characteristic of the solution to the problem but rather a process of adapting the organization to its environment.

References

Applied Data Research, Inc. *EMPIRE Modeling, Reporting, and Analysis System: An Introduction.* Princeton, N.J.: Applied Data Research, Inc., 1978.
Bloomfield, S. D. "Comprehensive Faculty Flow Analysis." In D. S. P. Hopkins and R. G. Schroeder (Eds.), *New Directions for Institutional Research: Applying Analytical Methods to Planning and Management,* no. 13. San Francisco: Jossey-Bass, 1977.
Bloomfield, S. D., and Updegrove, D. A. "An American Modeling System in Europe." *Journal of Institutional Management in Higher Education,* 1981, *5* (2).
Dickmeyer, N., Hopkins, D. S. P., and Massy, W. F. "TRADES: A Model for Interactive Financial Planning." *Business Officer,* 1978, *11* (9), 22–27.
Dresch, S. P. "A Critique of Planning Models for Postsecondary Education: Current Feasibility, Potential Relevance, and a Prospectus for Further Research." *Journal of Higher Education,* 1975, *46* (1), 245–286.
Greenberger, M., Crenson, M. A., and Crissey, B. L. *Models in the Policy Process.* New York: Russell Sage Foundation, 1976.
Hopkins, D. S. P. "On the Use of Large-Scale Simulation Models for University Planning." *Review of Educational Research,* 1971, *41* (5), 467–478.
Hopkins, D. S. P., and Massy, W. F. *Planning Models for Colleges and Universities.* Stanford, Calif.: Stanford University Press, 1981.
Jones, A. M., and Updegrove, D. A. "The EDUCOM Financial Planning Model: In Use Over EDUNET." Paper presented at CAUSE '78 National Conference, New Orleans, Dec. 1978.
Jones, A. M., Merrill, L. A., and Orcutt, R. L. *EFPM Documentation for Users.* Princeton, N.J.: EDUCOM, 1980.

Keen, P. G. W. "The Evolving Concept of Optimality." In M. K. Starr and M. Zeleny (Eds.), *Multi-Criteria Decision Making.* TIMS Studies in the Management Sciences, No. 6. New York: Elsevier North-Holland, 1977.

Keen, P. G. W. "Decision Support Systems: Translating Analytic Techniques into Useful Tools." *Sloan Management Review,* Spring 1980, *21* (2), 33–44.

Kemeny, J. G. "What Every College President Should Know About Mathematics." *The American Mathematical Monthly,* 1973, *80* (8), 889–901.

Knodle, L. L., and others. "EFPM: Users' Experiences at Purdue, Oberlin, and Carnegie-Mellon." *EDUCOM Bulletin,* Summer 1979, *14* (2), 5–11.

Lee, D. B. "Requiem for Large-Scale Models." *Journal of the American Institute of Planners,* 1973, *39* (3), 163–178.

Lindblom, C. E. "The Science of Muddling Through." *Public Administration Review,* 1959, *19,* 79–88.

March, J. G. "The Technology of Foolishness." *Civilokomen,* 1971, *18* (4), 4–12.

Mason, T. R. (Ed.). *New Directions for Institutional Research: Assessing Computer-Based Systems Models,* no. 9. San Francisco: Jossey-Bass, 1976.

Midwest Research Institute. *PLANTRAN II: Computer-Based Institutional Research and Planning.* Kansas City, Mo.: Midwest Research Institute, 1972.

Personal Software Inc. *VISICALC Computer Software Program.* Sunnyvale, Calif.: Personal Software Inc., 1979.

Planning Management Services Group. *Management Analysis and Planning Support System User Manual.* Little Rock, Ark.: Planning Management Services Group, 1979.

Plourde, P. "Institutional Use of Models: Hope or Continued Frustration?" In T. R. Mason (Ed.), *New Directions for Institutional Research: Assessing Computer-Based Systems Models,* no. 9. San Francisco: Jossey-Bass, 1976.

Schroeder, R. G. "Management Systems Design: A Critical Approach." In D. S. P. Hopkins and R. G. Schroeder (Eds.), *New Directions for Institutional Research: Applying Analytical Methods to Planning and Management,* no. 13. San Francisco: Jossey-Bass, 1977.

Simon, H. A. "A Behavioral Model of Rational Choice." In H. A. Simon (Ed.), *Models of Man.* New York: Wiley, 1957.

Strauss, J. C., Porter, R., and Zemsky, R. "Modeling and Planning at the University of Pennsylvania." In J. Wyatt, J. Emery, and C. Landis (Eds.), *Financial Planning Models: Concepts and Case Studies in Colleges and Universities.* Princeton, N.J.: EDUCOM, 1979.

Updegrove, D. A. "The Potential of a Shared Modeling System for Measurement of Comparative Financial Condition." Paper presented at ACE–NACUBO–NCES Working Conference on Measuring Financial Conditions of Colleges and Universities, Annapolis, Oct. 1978.

Updegrove, D. A. "EFPM: A Two-Year Progress Report." In *Planning for Computing: Proceedings of the 1980 EDUCOM National Conference.* Princeton, N.J.: EDUCOM, 1981.

Watkins, B. T. "How Stanford Uses Computer for Financial Modeling." *The Chronicle of Higher Education,* March 17, 1980, *20* (3), 3.

Wyatt, J. B., Emery, J. C., and Landis, C. P. (Eds.). *Financial Planning Models: Concepts and Case Studies in Colleges and Universities.* Princeton, N.J.: EDUCOM, 1979.

Wyatt, J. B., and Zeckhauser, S. H. "University Executives and Management Information: A Tenuous Relationship." *Educational Record,* 1975, *56* (3), 175–189.

Daniel A. Updegrove is director of planning model activities at EDUCOM, a Princeton, New Jersey-based nonprofit organization of 325 colleges and universities. He has lectured and consulted widely on the design and application of computer-based models.

*Although efforts to improve college management and information systems
are increasing in number and type, only recently have frameworks emerged
that also include management training needs and institutional change
strategies. One particular research-based framework is described.*

Planning for Improved Management

Edward P. St. John

Management development is a young, rapidly growing subfield in higher education. In recent years, there has been a flood of literature proposing new
approaches to planning systems (Kieft, Armijo, and Bucklew, 1978), information systems (Baldridge and Tierney, 1979; Bassett, 1979), and strategies for
improving training programs for college administrators (Argyris, 1980; Mayhew and others, 1974; and Webster and Shorthouse, 1976). Until recently,
however, there have been few frameworks to help guide administrators' decisions about the types of systems and training that they are likely to need.

Based on recent research on long-term management improvement
efforts at developing colleges and universities (St. John, 1980; St. John and
Weathersby, 1980), this chapter outlines a model of evolutionary change in
the organizational structure and management practices in colleges and universities. Then interventions are proposed that consider both formal management and information systems and less formal management training needs
and institutional change strategies. The general model used to develop these
interventions assumes that management needs are closely tied to the characteristics and history of a given institution. Therefore, the management interventions that have the greatest likelihood of success are those that are compatible with local needs. Fortunately, the increased emphasis on college management during the past decade has given higher education executives many

N. Poulton (Ed.). *New Directions for Institutional Research: Evaluation of Management and Planning Systems*, no. 31.
San Francisco: Jossey-Bass, September 1981

72

planning and management systems and management training programs from which to choose.

The General Model

The model was derived from theories of industrial organization and management, particularly traditional management theory, which includes both formal organizational structure and the general process of management (Massie, 1965). Management theorists argue that changes in formal organizational structure are closely linked to changes in the appropriate management practice, and that the formal structure largely determines the management practice that should be in place at a given time (Chandler, 1962; Greiner, 1972). This position has proved relevant to the study of college and university management (Bassett, 1979; Weathersby, 1975).

The analysis of several case studies leads to a general evolutionary model of five phases, with each phase associated with increased size and complexity (St. John, 1977; St. John, 1981). As colleges develop structurally, distinctively different organizational forms emerge, each building on the characteristics of the past. During the initial phase, structure is simple, the college is usually run by one or two key administrators, and development focuses on creating academic programs. As the institution grows into the second phase, administration becomes more formalized, some differentiation of administrative and academic functions occurs, and the focus of the organization shifts to maintaining programs and to defining long-range directions. During the third phase, functions added during the second phase are formalized into organizational subunits, and new subunits — schools, colleges, or campuses — are added. Management functions are delegated to subunits that are responsible for particular areas.

In the fourth phase, a more complex structure develops with systemwide administration of service units and a separate policy formulation function. Development focuses on central coordination of the activities of many diverse departments and subunits. The fifth phase is more speculative because the evidence is not yet complete (St. John, 1980). During this phase, there are tendencies toward an integrated or matrix structure that facilitates decentralized management. Systemwide administration and subunits collaborate through teams on policy formulation and implementation.

In a nongrowth era, this model is particularly useful in differentiating the management needs of different campus situations. It suggests that an effectively managed institution would have a management system compatible with its phase of structural development, and that certain management interventions are more appropriate to some organizational settings than others.

Case study analysis suggests a few tentative measures that might indicate or predict phases of structural development. Table 1 proposes four possible indicators and suggests ranges for each. In reality, a given institution may not

Table 1. Indicators of Structural Development
for Colleges and Universities

Phases	1 Creation	2 Direction	3 Delegation	4 Coordination	5 Collaboration
Enrollment (FTE)	0→600	600→1,800	1,800→5,000	5,000→20,000	Over 20,000
Central Administrators	1→5	5→10	10→15	15→25	Over 25
Colleges/Schools	1	1→3	3→7	7→14	Over 15
Campuses	1	1	1→2	1→3	4 or more

Source: Adapted from St. John and Weathersby, 1980.

fall exactly into these expected ranges. Within the cases studied, there were many exceptions. Any given institution might have two or three out of the four characteristics within the predicted range. Furthermore, these quantitative measures need to be supplemented with information about the institution's history, structure, and management.

In order to plan adequately for improved administrative practices, colleges need to undertake adequate needs assessments, which are often missing from management intervention practices in higher education (Baldridge and Tierney, 1979). The history of a college—particularly the development of the formal organization and management system—is an essential element of an adequate needs assessment. Once a needs assessment has been accomplished, it is possible for administrators to plan for improved administrative practices and formal management systems.

Interventions

Each of the institutions included in the original study (St. John, 1977; 1981), received funds from the Advanced Institutional Development Program (AIDP). AIDP gave each institution a large grant, usually $1 million to $3 million, to undertake comprehensive three- to five-year change efforts in curriculum, student affairs, and administrative areas. In short, these were total renewal efforts involving a number of interventions.

The term intervention is used in this discussion to indicate a set of structural activities directed toward organizational improvement. The case study research reported here concentrated on four kinds of interventions: formal management systems, management information systems, management training needs, and institutional change strategies. In practice, evidence indicates there is a close relationship between types of interventions that are implemented and types of administrative practices that are necessary to utilize the results.

Formal Management. Table 2 presents a brief summary of the management systems needs one can reasonably expect to find at institutions in the five developmental phases. The general concept of a formal institutional management system is divided into four component systems: planning, management, evaluation, and inquiring systems. These components are defined as follows: Planning systems refer to procedures for systematic institutional and program planning; management systems refer to day-to-day decision systems; evaluation systems refer to systems for evaluating progress toward planned (and possibly unplanned) outcomes; and inquiring systems refer to the data bases and information retrieval systems used by the other three systems. All of the institutions included in the original study were funded to undertake development efforts in these areas. Consequently, all of the case institutions had experimented with these management components. Combined, these four components of an institutional management system suggest a useful scheme for systematically categorizing institutional management needs.

According to the model, each subsequent management development builds on the developments needed in the prior phase — each adding to the capacities developed in prior phases. In practice, attaining balance in the phase of structural development and the institutional-management system is a difficult task. It is very likely that one or another component of a campus management system may be underdeveloped.

In addition, there was evidence in the case studies to suggest that management needs emerge in a fashion similar to Maslow's needs hierarchy of individuals (1954); the needs of the prior stage must be met before a new set of needs emerges. The management systems described in Table 1, therefore, function as plateaus at which an institution's management system might be most effective. To reach the appropriate plateau, the management needs associated with prior developmental phases must also be met. If a college or university is undermanaged, which is typically the case in higher education, then unmet management needs may have to be addressed incrementally.

The development matrix in Table 2 can also be used as a diagnostic tool for interventions designed to improve institutional management. Once an institution's phase of structural development is determined using historical and quantitative information, then the matrix can be used systematically to identify management deficiencies by comparing the actual management developments at the institutions with those considered appropriate for institutions in that phase. If some of the components of the general management system seem underdeveloped, then the model can be used to identify targets for management development efforts. For external intervention programs designed to improve management in particular areas, this approach can be used as a diagnostic tool for deciding what types of proposals to fund. The objective of a long-term development program could be to raise the levels of these management components for institutions in particular structural phases to those levels identified by the model.

Table 2. Intervention Model: Development Matrix for Planning, Management, Evaluation, and Inquiring Systems

Phase	Planning	Management	Evaluation	Inquiring
1. Creation	Short-range program planning	Informal collaborative interaction, task-oriented management	Market studies, supply-demand studies, knowledge of educational trends	Informal, interpersonal, judgmental, consensual
2. Direction	Add: long-range planning capacity	Add: formal systems for maintaining existing programs	Add: assessment of program impact, student/faculty attitudes	Add: standard format reports of transactions; functional budgets; annual reports; some computerization
3. Delegation	Add: department- and college-based planning capacities	Add: delegate management responsibilities to administrative units; formalization of management policies and procedures	Add: assessment of subunit performance on stated objectives	Add: unit cost analysis; seeking comparative data on costs, work loads, and performance data; computers required
4. Coordination	Add: systemwide planning, priority- and goal-setting	Add: system of coordinating diverse subunit activities and initiating coordinated activities	Add: prioritizing and assessing competing systemwide objectives	Add: objectives expressed as programs (PPBS attempted); simulation models to evaluate alternatives; program cost analyses; extensive computerization
5. Collaboration[a]	Add: formal collaborative planning processes between functional and central administrations	Add: systems for showing management responsibilities between subunits and central administration; matrix management possible	Add: assessment of system achievement of combined subunit and central objectives	Add: decentralized information systems; evaluate policy impact on subunits; evaluate central policy options; extensive distributed computerized systems

[a]Phase 5 systems are speculative and have not been formally studied.
Source: Adapted from St. John and Weathersby, 1980.

MIS Development. The use of the five-phase structural development model provides a useful conceptual basis for identifying and grouping the management information systems (MIS) development needs of diverse higher education institutions. It also provides a framework for addressing those needs. The following discussion reviews the MIS development analysis in five areas: the applicability of MIS systems, appropriate computer environment, MIS development priorities, factors limiting MIS implementation, and factors encouraging MIS implementation. These areas are summarized in Table 3 for each institutional level in the structural development model.

Phase 1 colleges, with small enrollments and limited financial resources to devote to management development, are faced with basic issues when making decisions about administrative computing. Often basic operating systems such as student registration and grade reports can be managed efficiently in a manual mode. These schools often have a registrar or admissions officer who knows most students. However, when automation is necessary for financial or student record systems, external assistance rather than in-house development is usually the most cost-effective solution. For small campuses that are branches or large colleges or systems, these data processing needs can usually be handled by the parent campus or by the central administration. For single-campus institutions, contractual arrangements with a local university or a consulting firm may provide the most cost-effective solution to computerization problems.

Automation decisions are slightly more complex for the small Phase 2 college than for perhaps any other institutional group. They have automation needs, usually for both financial and student systems, but their needs are not so complex as to require sophisticated simulation models. They need simple operating systems that will cut back on administrative costs, rather than complex data-driven analysis systems that are costly (in terms of staff support) to maintain. A key guide for administrators at Phase 2 schools when choosing administrative software should be whether installation of the new systems will require collection and automation of more types of data than are actually needed to meet operating and planning needs. These basic student and financial data can provide the information necessary for relating personnel and program decisions to enrollment and cost information. Other types of information such as data about student and faculty attitudes can be gathered and analyzed on an ad hoc basic as necessary. Fortunately, there are usually a variety of hardware options available to small colleges in the initial stages of computerization: contractual arrangements, microcomputers, or network access in most states and regions in the United States. Decisions about computer hardware options should also take into account instructional computing needs.

Phase 3 colleges and universities have complex administrative data-processing needs. They also usually lack the financial resources, unless they are part of a large multicampus system, to maintain large, well-staffed computing facilities. They need basic operating systems as well as some more sophis-

Table 3. MIS Development Framework

Phase	Applicability of MIS Systems	Computer Environment	MIS Development Priorities	Factors Limiting Implementation	Factors Encouraging Implementation
1. Creation	Relevant in limited areas, particularly student records and financial management	Computer support for automated MIS beyond means of institution	Automation of a few systems as appropriate	Local environment not sufficient to develop and maintain automated systems	Contractual arrangements with other institutions or firms
2. Direction	MIS development likely in some areas (student records and finance) and considered relevant for systems in most areas	Some computer development likely; either small special-purpose machines or part of a network	Initial systems may be planned in several areas with student records, finance, research, and financial aid being priority areas	Numerous problems emerge related to developing new systems (from scratch or adapting old systems); personnel, money, and machine access are key problems	Develop computer access (contractual, mini-computer, or network access); identify most important MIS priorities
3. Delegation	MIS moderately well developed with mixture of automated and manual systems in most areas; automation relevant in most areas	Computing likely, either CPU mainframe (medium-sized machine), mix of small machines, or network access; instructional computing likely	Initial systems in operation in several areas and specific system development priorities well identified	Personnel for systems development key limitation; money and software limitations; specific hardware needs (disk space, terminals) possible limitations	Training students in systems development and programming helps with personnel limits; following overall systems development plan also important
4. Coordination	MIS moderately to well developed; automation relevant for most systems in all areas; operating systems probable in most areas	Active computer environment likely; large mainframe, operated as part of central computer network or mixture of network and local computers	Automation important in most areas. Priorities include change to on-line systems, modification of existing systems, as well as developing new systems	Personnel and money key limiting factors, especially finding personnel with specialized expertise necessary to modify and update existing systems	Staff allocation and training decisions critical; limited individuals with required expertise; training non-D.P. personnel to maintain and operate systems also important
5. Collaboration	Automated systems essential to management of system; centralized systems and distributed systems in production	Complex computer environments with distributed hardware and distributed data processing in diverse administrative subunits	Refinement and updating of systems already in production; data base maintenance important	Personnel the most critical problem—finding people to develop and maintain distributed data processing (D.P.) systems	Staff training and development; exchange personnel for training purposes and develop compatible data definitions and processing systems

ticated systems in areas such as student financial aid, general administrative services, and institutional planning and research. They also often need a capacity to relate financial data to student data, or to cross-check student records with financial aid information. This requires easy access to reliable up-to-date information. Institutional researchers often need easy access to diverse types of data to respond to internal and external inquiries. This situation is often further complicated by a lack of trained personnel such as programmers or analysts, and by problems retaining these people once they are hired. These colleges often need to train and employ students as a partial solution to their personnel needs; they also need to evaluate their computer hardware needs realistically. Access to a large network plus some local capability, as opposed to developing or purchasing all systems to operate on in-house computers, may be the most cost-effective alternative.

Large coordinated colleges and universities — Phase 4 institutions — have complex administrative computing environments. Most have already developed basic operating systems, but also need new sytems in other areas such as the physical plant or possibly a hospital, and often need to update their basic financial systems to accommodate increased demands. They can make use of student-flow and financial models that will help central administrators relate enrollment information to student enrollment patterns. Program budgeting or a financial planning model may have been attempted. However, staff limitations, especially training needs, often impede the development of new systems and slow the implementation of already developed ones. It is practical to train administrators and staff in functional units — colleges, campuses, student service divisions — in the maintenance of operating systems. For these schools, maintenance of administrative and academic computing systems (on one or multiple machines) requires paying attention to hardware costs. Often investment in small machines can save on hardware costs, if problems with system compatibility can be overcome.

The extremely large, Phase 5 campus or university system has a distinctly different set of administrative computing problems. In addition to supporting the multiple users and systems through a centralized system, the central computing facility also has to support or at least coordinate the activities of other administrative computing centers, campuses, hospitals, or research offices. MIS development priorities often include refining and updating existing systems, as well as developing specialized capabilities such as student-flow modeling and induced-course–load analysis. These more sophisticated systems are essential for cost-conscious management decisions, both by central administration and by campus administrators and college deans. Decisions about which systems should be operated centrally and which should be decentralized can be critical to administrators in both the central administration and major subunits. Staff training, both for central administrative personnel and operating-unit personnel, is important. Staff exchange programs between operating units and central administration are a definite possibility. System compatibility is also a major concern and, therefore, standardizing reporting dates and data-element definitions across subunits is important both for operations and management.

Management Training. In a review of the state of the art of management development and training in colleges and universities, Webster and Shorthouse (1976) identified a significant deficiency in professional training of higher-education administrators. Traditionally, colleges and universities have promoted people successful in their academic pursuits, usually with advanced training in a specialized academic field, to positions of leadership—department heads, academic deans, and presidents. Once promoted, these people usually have to rely on their native skills and instincts as well as the observations of the functioning of their institutions they made as graduate students and professors. They are often not initially equipped to deal with the complexities of financial stress now facing colleges, and historically there has been a shortage of both in-service and campus-based training programs for higher education managers and others (Mayhew, 1974; Webster and Shorthouse, 1976). Consequently, the management training program is an important intervention.

A management-development model can be used to suggest the types of management training that is most likely needed by an institution in a given phase. Table 4 suggests such a scheme. As in the case of formal management system development, each phase adds to and complements the developments of each prior phase. Management training needs obviously become more sophisticated as institutions increase in complexity.

According to this approach, the staff in institutions in all phases will need background and training that will help with curriculum and program development tasks when needed. These needs will be the strongest in Phase 1 institutions. In addition, top managers in Phase 2 institutions need management skills that will help them define the long-term direction of the institution and develop formal systems to maintain existing programs. The more complex Phase 3 institutions need training programs for middle managers—deans, department heads, and directors of administrative subunits—to improve their overall management skills. Phase 4 institutions will also need training programs for both academic and administrative managers who are involved in coordinating subunit activities. These institutions are likely to have a greater need for training in team-building techniques than those in prior phases, since coordination requires cooperation among key administrative personnel. Phase 5 institutions have to develop the support services required by decentralized organizations. While many administrative support services such as word processing or more formal planning and management functions are decentralized, it is still necessary for central administration to maintain certain support and coordinating services. In the computing area, central administrators need training in the design of decentralized systems and staff training techniques. In other administrative areas, such as academic program review and plan-

80

Table 4. Management Training Needs by Development Phase

Phase	Management Focus	Management Training
1.	Creating new programs	Staff training in problem solving, brainstorming, curriculum design, and program development
2.	Defining long-term direction and maintaining existing programs	Add: top management training in long-range planning techniques, system development, and formal accounting and personnel management procedures
3.	Delegating administrative responsibilities to organizational subunits	Add: training of middle managers in formal management techniques, including management-by-objectives and formal systems development
4.	Coordinating subunit activities	Add: training of academic and administrative managers in team-building techniques, systems and policy analysis, and priority- and and goal-setting techniques
5.	Collaborating among decentralized organizations	Add: training of central administrative personnel in systems maintenance, decentralized systems design, and consulting as support techniques

Source: Adapted from St. John and Weathersby, 1980.

ning, central administrators need training in policy planning and evaluation techniques.

This framework suggests only the types of management training that are likely to be encountered in institutions that are attempting to develop management systems. It does not suggest means for attaining these outcomes. There are increasing numbers of management training options available to higher education institutions, including consulting firms that provide campus-based training programs, and short-term institutes and workshops that take individuals away from the campus for short periods. This framework can be helpful to institutional administrators who are deciding which management training options to pursue.

Institutional Change Strategies. The analysis of the AIDP projects indicated that the types of change strategies that appeared most appropriate seemed to vary according to developmental phase, just as the effectiveness of different management systems varied according to developmental phase. A summary of these findings follows.

Phase 1 institutions are oriented toward the creation of programs and toward informal management systems. On the basis of these facts, one might predict that the most appropriate development strategies for these institutions would be oriented toward program planning and development. In fact, these were the primary management activities at Phase 1 institutions. Administrators and faculty in these schools need the freedom to develop new courses and programs.

Phase 2 institutions have more formal organizational structures and management systems than Phase 1 organizations. Consequently, an intensive institutional development effort should have some structure, yet allow for the informal and collaborative processes that take place in these organizations. In both Phase 2 institutions included in the original study, the same elements were present: A team of people took responsibility for implementing the project, and in each case strategies were developed to work changes into the system.

Phase 3 institutions have organizational structures that are more functionally differentiated than either Phase 1 or Phase 2 institutions. Therefore, greater management skills are required at middle-management levels. In Phase 3 institutions, an effective development strategy has to work through the delegated structure, thus involving middle managers in the implementation process. In the two case studies of Phase 3 institutions, the development strategies involved middle managers in the change process. In less complex organizations, involving middle managers is not as crucial to the change process.

At Phase 4 institutions, the primary management development task of developing coordinating capacity is even more complex. These institutions need change strategies that involve representatives from functional subunits in the implementation of new activities that affect their operations. As in Phase 3 institutions, individuals take responsibility for the implementation of specific activities. However, coordinators are more likely to be part of the central administration than middle managers. In the two Phase 4 institutions studied, the implementation process seemed to progress most effectively when central administrators took responsibility for implementing specific activities.

Phase 5 institutions require collaborative approaches to the task of institutional development. Successful change strategies would probably accommodate a decentralized decision structure. Systemwide innovations must utilize existing, often decentralized resources. One apparently effective strategy is to use planning teams (with representative membership) as a means of attaining an appropriate balance between decentralized services and centralized support. In the computing area, for example, such a strategy would involve decentralizing hardware decisions while centralizing some planning and support functions (Norris and St. John, 1980).

Improvement of college management systems is an increasingly important and complex issue facing most college administrators. As enrollment growth has slowed, and the financial conditions of colleges has become more stressful, administrators have increasingly turned to sophisticated management systems as a means of improving their decision capacity. However, a decade of management improvement efforts has proven that while formal management can improve college administrative practice, it can also lead to

82

implementation of systems that are more sophisticated than are actually necessary (Baldridge and Tierney, 1979; St. John, 1981).

Colleges can avoid the pitfall of implementing systems that are not appropriate if adequate needs assessments are undertaken. When planning for improved management, administrators must recognize that management needs are closely tied to the structure and history of their organizations, and that planning for formal planning, management, and information systems should be accompanied by planning for the training needs of faculty and administrators who are the implementors and users of these systems. In addition, the types of institutional change strategies that are utilized when planning for improved management should take into account these same organizational factors.

References

Argyris, C. "Educating Administrators and Professionals." In C. Argyris and R. M. Cyert, *Leadership in the '80s: Essays on Higher Education.* Cambridge, Mass.: Institute for Educational Management, Harvard University, 1980.

Baldridge, J. V., and Tierney, M. L. *New Approaches to Management.* San Francisco: Jossey-Bass, 1979.

Bassett, R. *Postsecondary Education Information at the State Level: Planning Guide.* Boulder, Colo: National Center for Higher Education Management Systems, 1979.

Chandler, A. D. *Strategy and Structure: Chapters in the History of the Industrial Enterprise.* Cambridge, Mass.: M.I.T. Press, 1962.

Greiner, L. E. "Evolution and Revolution as Organizations Grow." *Harvard Business Review,* 1972, *50,* 37–46.

Kieft, R. N., Armijo, F., and Bucklew, N. S. *A Handbook for Institutional Academic and Program Planning: From Idea to Implementation.* Boulder, Colo: National Center for Higher Education Management Systems, 1978.

Maslow, A. H. *Motivation and Personality.* New York: Harper & Row, 1954.

Massie, J. L. "Management Theory." In J. G. March (Ed.), *Handbook of Organizations.* Chicago: Rand McNally, 1965.

Mayhew, L. B., and the Committee on Administration and Policy Analysis. *Educational Leadership and Declining Enrollments.* Berkeley, Calif.: McCutchan, 1974.

Norris, D. M., and St. John, E. P. "New Directions in Statewide Computer Planning and Cooperation." Paper presented at annual meeting of the Society for College and University Planning, Quebec, Aug. 1980.

St. John, E. P. *Structure, Management, and Intervention: Final Report. A Study of Selected Developing Colleges and Universities.* Washington, D.C.: Office of Planning, Budgeting, and Evaluation, U.S. Office of Education, 1977.

St. John, E. P. "A Framework for MIS Development in Higher Education." *CAUSE/ EFFECT,* 1980, *3* (4), 24–31.

St. John, E. P. *Public Policy and College Management: A Study of Selected Developing Colleges and Universities.* New York: Praeger, 1981.

St. John, E. P., and Weathersby, G. B. "Management Development in Higher Education: Intervention Strategies for Developing Colleges and Universities." *International Journal of Institutional Management in Higher Education,* 1980, *4* (2), 105–119.

Weathersby, G. B. "Decision Paradigms and Models for Higher Education." Paper presented at 48th meeting of the Institute of Management Sciences and the Operations Research Society of America, November 1975.

Webster, R. S., and Shorthouse, B. O. *The State of the Art of Management Development and Training and a Model for These Activities in Colleges and Universities.* Coconut Grove, Fla.: Higher Education Management Institute, 1976.

Edward P. St. John is currently a visiting faculty member at the Institute for Higher Education, University of New England, Armidale, N.S.W., Australia. Formerly he was a higher education policy specialist for the Office of Planning and Budget, U.S. Department of Education, and associate director of research and planning, Missouri Department of Higher Education.

*Several guidelines are available to help both the executive officer
and the practitioner assess the evolution of management
and planning systems.*

Assessing Management and
Planning Systems

Nick L. Poulton

This sourcebook began the discussion of management and planning systems
by posing four questions: What are current practices? What are the impacts of
these practices? What conditions contribute to these impacts? And how can
the institutional research and/or planning practitioner monitor impacts as they
occur? In dealing with these questions, the authors of this volume present a
common theme about the "problem" of management and planning systems—
namely, that the major issue surrounding management and planning in colleges and universities is not the absence of ideal models for guiding management practices, planning processes, or information techniques for decision
making. The problem is the development of a strategy for moving university
decision making toward a practice of developing rational bases for decision
making and using these bases to explain decisions.

This assessment presents a summary of the themes and observations
offered by the authors as they discussed various management and planning
techniques. The summary is developed with the institutional researcher in
mind and includes suggestions on how researchers may assess changes in the
management practices of their institutions.

Impacts

The authors have cited a wide array of impacts and outcomes, some
positive, some negative, some very specific, and some general. Taken collec-

N. Poulton (Ed.). *New Directions for Institutional Research: Evaluation of Management and Planning Systems*, no. 31.
San Francisco: Jossey-Bass, September 1981

tively, the primary products of the management and planning systems discussed in this volume are twofold: improved ability to store and analyze information and improved bases for taking action.

Improved Information. The continued improvement of management information is evident in many forms. New vantage points are available for systematic, structured introspection into the units and environment of colleges and universities. Problems are better understood. Better questions are asked. More alternatives are considered. Information is stored and analyzed in ways that generate new ideas for improving the institution. Sharing information promotes better communication in the organization. The quality of discussion and debate increases. And all of these factors contribute to administrative action.

Basis for Action. The ultimate contribution of management and planning systems is legitimizing the basis upon which administrators and constituents take action. The discussions of management practices in this volume report that several common features contribute to successful results. These include openness and sharing of information and problems identified through planning and institutional research, expanded participation of constituents in the decision-making process, and commitment of talented leaders to directing information, participants, and issues toward action. Achieving these conditions maintains the underlying elements of trust, confidence, and legitimacy upon which administrators are able to act. Management systems and planning practices add the rationale to the developed information bases for decision making, and the probability increases that better decisions will be made in a more timely fashion.

Negative Impacts. Unfortunately, the efforts to develop management and planning systems are not always successful. The present conditions of limited resources in colleges and universities do not allow for the traditional rewards of increased resources for the productive involvement of people in planning and decision-making processes. Typically, as information improves and meaningful participation takes place, the quality of arguments for additional resources also improves. Then expectations are raised based not only on these better arguments, but also simply on the belief that a good-faith effort deserves a just reward. Frustrations of a different kind may emerge when participants are not able to observe the often subtle influences, rather than the infrequently dramatic results, of master-planning discussions, since these activities typically involve many people and are very complex and broad. In the extreme situation of severe retrenchment involving program and personnel reductions, there is never enough time or sufficient rationale for supporting these decisions. A functioning management and planning system must be in place and well developed prior to severe resource crisis, for it will be taxed to the limit and beyond. Given the combined problems of limited rewards, frustrated participants, and limited means of communicating with all members of the institution, the credibility of all management and planning systems is continually threatened. Consequently, the impacts per se are not necessarily as important to the practitioner as the conditions in the organization that contribute to the desired impacts.

Conditions Affecting Impacts

The attention to conditions affecting sources of planning and management sytems has shifted over the past decade from technical design considerations to the administrative and organizational environment. Technical design matters such as the design of a management information system, the content of a master plan, the elements of a management-by-objectives system, or the usual steps in a program review process have all been well developed and tested, as reported by the authors of this volume.

Given that the technical considerations, including the adequacy of resources, are reasonably well satisfied, the authors focus on factors of the administrative environment as determining whether a planning and management system will change the decision-making behavior of a college or university. Taken collectively, the primary factors are: needs assessment, top executive commitment and involvement, and the participation and receptivity of constituents. These are not new realizations, for they have been included in similar observations elsewhere (Baldridge, 1980; Poulton, 1980). But they are sufficiently important to warrant continuing discussion.

Needs Assessment. Although the clarification of problems seems such a logical first step, it is often overlooked. An institution and its environment must be carefully diagnosed, for different management and planning activities serve different needs and different users. A productive match between user and activity necessitates an understanding of both. In the preceding chapter, St. John presents a way of viewing institutions at different levels of structural development. The requirements for a given planning activity differ according to these levels. Too often, key administrators and some institutional researchers as well have a personal diagnosis that may not be shared or at worst may be inaccurate. Consequently, potential users and the decision questions they face must be identified, and their decision-making behavior and information needs must be analyzed. Basic purposes must be stated and understood by participants, then restated, reinforced, and refined. As projects evolve, organizational memory tends to dim. But ultimately, the perceived utility of management and planning systems depends upon a fairly close match between the decision maker's needs, the kinds of information provided, and the nature of the issues addressed.

Assessment Questions. Are needs reviewed periodically? Is a recognized match developing between product and user?

Executive Commitment. Virtually every author cites top-level executive commitment as the primary ingredient of institutional readiness for developing a management or planning system. Furthermore, if the users are executive officers, then they need to be involved in the needs assessment and in all phases of project design, implementation, and evaluation. The most effective products and processes are those that are based upon the principles that also guide the behavior of key decision makers. However, commitment to act is all-important. Earlier in this volume, Kent Caruthers described the necessity "to determine whether decisions are being made or being avoided." Depending upon this latter condition, a management or planning activity could flow from the principles guiding administrative behavior or could be intervening to change those guiding principles. The administrative environment is more compatible in the first case and more problematic in the second.

Assessment Questions. Are decisions being made or avoided? Are principles guiding administrative behavior a primary target of change?

Participation. A common principle underlying management and planning sytems development in most colleges and universities is a commitment to constituent partipation through direct involvement, observation, or communication. Greater success is likely when careful attention is given to learning from and communicating with participants and evolving a mutually understood division of labor among participants. The direct participant must not undertake responsibilities exceeding his or her time, expertise, and interest. The observer requires a genuinely open, collaborative administrative climate that does not demand specific products but remains open to productive suggestions. All other constituents need the option to inform themselves about management and planning activities. Those activities that are fairly well integrated with decision-making processes occur in institutions where administrators have a heightened awareness of the need for regular, multichannel communication with all constituents. All of this requires effort and time for the differing roles to develop. Particularly important is the evolution of a supportive division of labor between administrative staff and advisory groups of constituents. Given an open operating style, mutual trust can emerge. If it is also apparent that continuing consultation and cooperation influence the design and substance of a management or planning activity, then adivsory group members are usually satisfied with their part-time advisory roles, for they also become acquainted with the complex, time-consuming set of tasks that require the full-time commitment of administrative staff.

Assessment Question: Is there a supporting and influential division of labor between administrative staff and advisory groups?

Evolution of Management and Planning

All facets of the organization evolve continuously. This overrides all the conditions regarding the contributions of management and planning systems to organizational improvement. Obviously, the problems facing a university change as crises arise and dissolve, and they may divert attention away from the longer-range commitment to improve management and planning behavior. But other features also change. New people arrive with different ideas, skills, and talents. Organizational structures are revised. Felt needs change as different questions regarding university operations are asked and in turn raise new demands for information. Activities are adjusted to be more economical. Some initially intended projects are postponed or discarded as workloads expand. Images of management and planning are transient, and rhetoric requires renewal in order to maintain visibility and commitment. Some of these changes are necessary, some are inevitable, and others are wholly unexpected. Amid these changes, the causality among decision needs, activity type, and administrative style does not appear to be a critical issue, for all three elements evolve mutually. Management and planning processes evolve to meet specific needs and to incorporate particular administrative styles. Decision makers' perspectives change to include important issues highlighted through these processes. The important point for the institutional researcher is the need to keep experimenting with projects and processes so that opportunities to add them to management practices can be seized when they occur.

As stated earlier, the trend in management and planning systems development has been toward greater attention to the administrative environment. The institutional researcher needs to be increasingly acquainted with this topic. One source of help in matching activities to users is information concerning the evolutionary growth and development of organizations first researched in the business world (Gluck, Kaufman, and Walleck, 1980) and applied to colleges and universities by St. John and Weathersby (1980). In their research on successful business corporations, Gluck, Kaufman, and Walleck (1980) constructed a four-phase evolutionary model having strategic management as the last phase. The value system shared by top and middle managers in strategically managed companies contains four elements that could serve the higher education enterprise as well. They are:

1. "The values of teamwork, which leads to task-oriented organizational flexibility
2. Entrepreneurial drive, or the commitment to making things happen
3. Open communication, rather than the preservation of confidentiality
4. A shared belief that the enterprise can largely create its own future, rather than be buffeted into a predetermined corner by the winds of environmental change" (p. 160).

References

Baldridge, J. V. "Managerial Innovation—Rules for Successful Implementation." *Journal of Higher Education,* 1980, *51* (2), 117–134.
Gluck, F. W., Kaufman, S. P., and Walleck, A. S. "Strategic Management for Competitive Advantage." *Harvard Business Review,* 1980, *58* (4), 154–161.
Poulton, N. L. "Strategies of Large Universities." In P. Jedamus, M. W. Peterson, and Associates, *Improving Academic Management: A Handbook of Planning and Institutional Research.* San Francisco: Jossey-Bass, 1980.

St. John, E. P., and Weathersby, G. B. "Management Development in Higher Education: Intervention Strategies for Developing Colleges and Universities." *International Journal of Institutional Management in Higher Education,* 1980, *4* (2), 105–119.

Nick L. Poulton is director of university planning at Western Michigan University.

Contributing authors describe what they consider the best two or three references in their topic areas.

Useful References

The contributing authors have identified the two or three references in their respective topic areas that they would most recommend for further study. These are organized below in the same order as the chapters in this volume. The brief annotations are provided so that readers may select the most useful source with the least amount of time and effort.

Environmental Assessments

Cope, R. G. *Strategic Policy Planning: A Guide for College and University Administrators.* Littleton, Colo.: Ireland Educational Corporation, 1978.

    This reference provides a full treatment of strategic planning concepts as they apply to higher education. It is intended as a practical guide to both the planning concept, which the author describes as a "way of thinking," and the planning process.

Hofer, C. W., and Schendel, D. *Strategy Formulation: Analytical Concepts.* St. Paul, Minn.: West Publishing, 1978.

    The concept of strategic planning, virtually all of the practice, and most of the research come from the business community. This single reference contains a full treatment of the state of the art. It offers an excellent summary of the literature with practical illustrations from many types of organizations, both profit and nonprofit.

N. Poulton (Ed.). *New Directions for Institutional Research: Evaluation of Management and Planning Systems,* no. 31. San Francisco: Jossey-Bass, September 1981

Master Plans

Caruthers, J. K., and Lott, G. B. *Mission Review: Foundation for Strategic Planning.* Boulder, Colo.: National Center for Higher Education Management Systems, 1981.

Along with analysis of institutional capabilities and identification of external opportunities and constraints, this reference contributes to the formulation of strategic plans. The importance of a well-understood sense of mission as the basis for strategic planning is emphasized. In addition, *Mission Review* traces the history of planning for colleges and universities, discusses the content of mission statements, and describes seven considerations that must be addressed in developing a master plan. An appendix focuses on state-level master planning.

Reddick, D. C. *Wholeness and Renewal in Education: A Learning Experience at Austin College.* Sherman, Tex.: Center for Program and Institutional Renewal, 1979.

The unique development of a master plan for Austin College involved the transformation of the entire institution. This chronicle of the experience shows that self-renewal, as a concept analogous to master planning, must be continuous, based on a clear understanding of goals, and built into the routine functions and processes of the college. In particular, this case indicates that self-renewal mechanisms must function at three levels — those of the individual, the program, and the institution as a whole.

Shirley, R. C., and Volkwein, J. F. "Establishing Academic Program Priorities." *Journal of Higher Education,* 1978, *49* (5), 472–488.

An approach to strategic planning is developed for academic institutions facing retrenchment. Particular attention is paid to the matching process through which internal strengths and weaknesses; external needs, opportunities, and constraints; and institutional mission are brought together to focus on decisions about program offerings and priorities. Three broad categories of evaluative criteria are offered: quality, need, and cost.

Resource Allocations

Anthony, R. N., Deardon, J., and Vancil, F. R. *Management Control Systems.* Homewood, Ill.: Richard D. Irwin, 1972.

Anthony, R. N., and Herzlinger, R. E. *Management Control in Nonprofit Organizations.* Homewood, Ill.: Richard D. Irwin, 1975.

These volumes carefully distinguish among the functions of strategic planning, management control, and operational control. Although the orientation is toward the profit sector, the second volume applies to colleges and universities.

Caruthers, J. K., and Orwig, M. *Budgeting in Higher Education.* AAHE–ERIC Higher Education Research Report No. 3. Washington, D.C.: American Association for Higher Education, 1979.

This monograph provides a comprehensive review of budgeting within colleges and universities as well as at the state level. Particularly useful is the authors' analysis of current approaches to budgeting in postsecondary education.

Zemsky, R., Porter, R., and Oedel, L. P. "Decentralized Planning: To Share Responsibility." *Educational Record,* 1979, *59,* 229–253.

An objective, introspective analysis is provided of the impact of one approach to responsibility center management within a complex university. The need to preserve academic values in the decision-making process is emphasized.

Program Reviews

Anderson, S. B., and Ball, S. *The Profession and Practice of Program Evaluation.* San Francisco: Jossey-Bass, 1978.

This volume introduces the basic issues of program evaluation. While not treating each issue in depth, it provides a comprehensive introduction and framework for the concepts, methods, and ethical issues in the field. Its relevance for those involved in postsecondary program reviews lies in the professional context it provides for the practice of program review.

Barak, R. J., and Berdahl, R. O. *State-Level Academic Program Review.* Report No. 107. Denver: In-Service Education Program, Education Commission of the States, February 1978.

Melchiori, G. S. *Pattern of Program Discontinuance: A Comparative Analysis of State Agency Procedures for Initiating and Implementing the Discontinuance of Academic Programs.* Research report. Ann Arbor: Center for the Study of Higher Education, University of Michigan, 1980.

These two research reports present national information on state-level program reviews and their impact on postsecondary institutions. Both reports go beyond offering interesting facts by analyzing trends, identifying inadequacies, offering suggestions, and conceptualizing the processes institutions use to cope with state-initiated program reviews.

Heydinger, R. B. "Does Our Institution Need Program Review?"
Mims, R. S. "Program Review and Evaluation: Designing and Implementing the Review Process." (ERIC ED 192 629)
Poulton, N. L. "Program Review and Evaluation: Integrating Results into Decision Making." (ERIC ED 181 791)

These three papers were prepared as an integrated presentation at the annual Forum of the Association for Institutional Research, Houston, May

94

21–25, 1978. They provide an insightful institution-level analysis of the program review process. They include investigating the need for program review, designing and implementing it, and utilizing its results. Academic leaders considering program reviews and institutional researchers practicing them will find many helpful concepts and suggestions.

Computer Models

Greenberger, M., Crenson, M. A., and Crissey, B. L. *Models in the Policy Process.* New York: Russell Sage Foundation, 1976.
 This volume presents a wide-ranging survey and analysis of the impacts of computer models on public policy formulation and evaluation. Although modeling in higher education is not covered specifically, both the broad overview and the specific studies of systems dynamnics, econometric modeling, and the New York City/Rand Institute's attempts to model public service delivery systems are of interest. Especially insightful is the treatment of the often conflicting roles of the modeler and the policy maker.

Hopkins, D. S. P., and Massy, W. F. *Planning Models for Colleges and Universities.* Stanford, Calif.: Stanford University Press, 1981.
 The uses and misuses of planning models and the principles for developing such models are discussed. Specific models that have proven useful at Stanford University and elsewhere are described. Models cover such problems as financial forecasting; estimating resource requirements and variable costs of programs; financial equilibrium; faculty appointment, promotion, and retirement; predicting student enrollments; and evaluating financial alternatives.

Keen, P. G. W. "The Evolving Concept of Optimality." In M. K. Starr and M. Zeleny (Eds.), *Multi-Criteria Decision Making.* TIMS Studies in the Management Sciences, no. 6. New York: Elsevier North-Holland, 1977.
 A critical survey is presented of both the prescriptive literature on optimization science (microeconomics, operations research, and systems analysis) and the descriptive literature on individual and organizational decision making. The problems of applying models to complex, multicriteria decision making are analyzed, and a solution is proposed, namely for decision makers to use interactive models themselves.

Wyatt, J. B., Emery, J. C., and Landis, C. P. (Eds.). *Financial Planning Models: Concepts and Case Studies in Colleges and Universities.* Princeton, N.J.: EDUCOM, 1979.
 In response to a recent survey of financial modeling, administrators at Carnegie-Mellon, Harvard, Lehigh, Oberlin, the University of Pennsylvania, Stanford, the State University of New York at Albany, and Yale describe their models and their usefulness. The development and early applications of the EDUCOM Financial Planning Model (EFPM) are also discussed.

Management Development

Argyris, C., and Cyert, R. M. *Leadership in the '80s: Essays on Higher Education.* Cambridge, Mass.: Institute for Educational Management, Harvard University, 1980.

Two noted organizational theorists discuss the management and training issues facing higher education administrators in the 1980s. Argyris's essay focuses on issues related to organized learning and the types of leadership training college and university administrators are likely to need to maximize effective management. Cyert's essay focuses more broadly on the diverse range of management issues and concludes that strong presidential leadership will be a requirement during the next decade.

Baldridge, J. V., and Tierney, M. L. *New Approaches to Management: Creating Practical Systems of Management Information and Management by Objectives.* San Francisco: Jossey-Bass, 1979.

Baldridge and Tierney identify proven strategies for implementing successful management information systems and management by objectives based upon their evaluation of the EXXON-sponsored Resource Allocation on Management Program (RAMP). This program was designed to bring sophisticated management practices to small and medium-sized colleges, to consider practical strategies for designing information systems, and to relate management information to financial allocation decisions. Although these practices were potentially helpful for planning and resource management, the authors conclude that the absence of adequate needs assessments is a major factor limiting success.

St. John, E. P. *Public Policy and College Management: A Study of Selected Developing Colleges and Universities.* New York: Praeger, 1981.

St. John uses in-depth case studies of five Title III-funded colleges and universities to develop a management intervention model. The model has direct implications for institutional management planning and for state and federal programs designed to improve college management systems, automated management information, management training, and institutional change strategies. The case studies are used to illustrate the ways these practices can be improved. Institutional management, information, and training needs vary according to the local environment and history. Successful strategies for improving planning and management systems consider local needs.

Index

A

Adams, D., 33, 41
Advanced Institutional Development Program (AIDP), 73, 80
American Association for Higher Education, 8
American Association of State Colleges and Universities, 8
American Council on Education, 8
Analytical support, for master planning, 24–25, 26
Anderson, S. B., 52, 59, 93
Anthony, R. N., 40, 41, 92
Applied Data Research, 64, 68
Aquinas College, master plan of, 21, 23, 24
Argyris, C., 71, 82, 95
Armijo, F., 71, 82
Arns, R. G., 53, 57, 59
Austin College, master plan of, 21, 23, 24, 92
Austin Peay State University, master plan of, 23
Australia, planning models in, 65

B

Bacchetti, R., 63
Balderston, F. E., 30, 41, 42
Baldridge, J. V., 31, 35, 39, 41, 71, 73, 82, 87, 89, 95
Ball, S., 93
Barak, R. J., 50–51, 53, 55–56, 59, 93
Bassett, R., 71, 72, 82
Belgium, planning models in, 65
Bell, C. H., Jr., 31, 42
Benacerraf, P., 31, 34, 41
Bennett, K. H., 37, 42
Berdahl, R. O., 50–51, 53, 55–56, 59, 93
Bloomfield, S. D., 63, 65, 68
Boggs, J. H., 21, 27
Boston College, environmental position of, 11
Boston University, environmental position of, 11–12

Brandeis University, environmental position of, 11
Bucklew, N. S., 71, 82
Budgeting: income-expense, 33, 36, 37–38; incremental, trends in, 32–33; zero-base, 33, 37, 40

C

California, public medical schools in, 12
Cammack, E. F., 30, 42
CAMPUS, 62
Canada, planning models in, 65
Carnegie Corporation, 1
Carnegie-Mellon University, planning model at, 65, 94
Caruthers, J. K., 2, 17–28, 32, 33, 37, 42, 88, 92, 93
Central Washington State College, in institutional market, 13
Chandler, A. D., 72, 82
Cheit, E. F., 31, 42
Clarkson College of Technology, responsibility center management at, 38
Clover Park Vocational-Technical, in institutional market, 13
Coles, C. D., 52, 59
Collaboration phase, in management development, 72–73, 75, 77–80, 81
Collier, D., 6, 15
Committee on Administration and Policy Analysis, 82
Communicating, and master plan, 25, 27
Computers. *See* Planning models
Connors, E. T., 33, 42
Coordination phase, in management development, 72–73, 75, 77–78, 79–80, 81
Cope, R. G., 2, 5–15, 91
Cornell University, and planning models, 64
Creation phase, in management development, 72–73, 75, 76–77, 79–81
Crenson, M. A., 62, 68, 94
Crissey, B. L., 62, 68, 94
Cyert, R. M., 33, 42, 95